MICHA   L

AMONGST
BARBARIANS

NICK HERN BOOKS

A division of Walker Books Limited

A Nick Hern Book

Amongst Barbarians first published in 1989 as an original paperback
by Nick Hern Books, a division of Walker Books Limited,
87 Vauxhall Walk, London SE11 5HJ

Amongst Barbarians copyright © 1989 by Michael Wall
Front cover: supernatural motif from a Sarawak longhouse
Copyright APA Photo Agency

Set in Baskerville by BookEns, Saffron Walden, Essex
Printed by Billings & Sons, Worcester

British Library Cataloguing in Publication Data
Wall, Michael
    Amongst Barbarians
    I. Title
    822'914
    ISBN 1-85459-015-4

Caution
All rights whatsoever in this play are strictly reserved. Requests to
reproduce the text in whole or in part should be addressed to the
publisher. Application for performance in any medium or for
translation into any language should be addressed to the author's
sole agent, Micheline Steinberg, 110 Frognal, London NW3 6XU.
No performance may be given unless a licence has been obtained.

Characters

BRYAN   Aged 20. From North London.

RALPH   Early twenties, possibly late twenties. English, but has a slightly Americanised accent.

GAOLER   Sikh. Large, tough man. Good English.

LAWYER   Tamil. Elegant woman in her thirties. Excellent English.

GEORGE   Bryan's father. North Londoner. Bad nerves.

WENDY   Bryan's mother. Aged early forties. Loud voice.

LILLY   Bryan's sister. Aged 17–19. Heavy. Young mother.

TONI   Ralph's mother. Aged 40, perhaps older. Glamorous.

BARMAN   Young Malay or Chinese. Attractive to the women.

The setting

Penang, Malaysia, at the present time.

Two hotel bedrooms; a bar; a prison cell.

Amongst Barbarians was first staged at the Royal Exchange Theatre, Manchester on 9 February 1989. The cast was as follows:

BRYAN	Dominic Keating
RALPH	Ronan Vibert
GAOLERS	Tariq Yunus
	Zubie Dar
	Anji Dar
LAWYER	Sakuntala Ramanee
GEORGE	Christopher Hancock
WENDY	Avril Elgar
LILLY	Kathy Burke
TONI	Rosalind March
BARMAN	Ricardo Sibelo

Directed by James Maxwell
Designed by David Millard
Lighting by Vincent Herbert
Sound by Alastair Goolden
Fights Director Nicholas Hall

This text went to press before the opening night, and may therefore differ slightly from the text as performed.

ACT ONE

Scene One

Prison cell in Penang, Malaysia.
It should be brightly-lit and spacious – white walls, hot. If possible, signs of
life behind the cell, where other prisoners occupy a sort of open area.
BRYAN and RALPH have come in. They are dejected, exhausted. BRYAN
is 20; RALPH is older. RALPH slumps on his bed. He has a Sony
Walkman. BRYAN seems lost. He presents an incongruous sight here, and
indeed he has little idea of where he is or what's happened to him.
Silence for a while.

BRYAN. Well that's us nicely bolloxed, ennit?

> RALPH *says nothing.*

—Very nicely bolloxed. Thank you very much. Oi—I'm talking
to you.

RALPH. Yeah.

BRYAN. Oh you can hear me; I thought you couldn't hear. I
thought perhaps you had that wonderful instrument you call
brain switched off.

RALPH. I can hear you.

BRYAN. Well that's something.
That fucking persecutor, he made it all up didn't he? We
never done half the things he said we done. Well, *I* never; I
dunno what *you* done.

RALPH. Prosecutor.

BRYAN. What?

RALPH. It's prosecutor, not persecutor, although I suppose . . .
(*He stops.*)

BRYAN. Bollocks.

RALPH. Yeah well why don't you try and give things their proper
names, you know?

BRYAN. I'll give you your proper name, pal.

RALPH. All right.

BRYAN. All right.
I mean they took no notice about that copper, did they? The one in charge who—what's'isname—solicited, the one who solicited the 20,000 dollars. That's a fucking bribe he was trying to get—I dunno what else you'd call it. They failed to take that into account.

RALPH. They did.

BRYAN. What?

RALPH. They did take it into account.

BRYAN. What?

RALPH. What d'you mean 'what'?

BRYAN. When?

RALPH. It's a separate issue. It's got nothing to do with our guilt or innocence.

BRYAN. 'Course it's got to do with it!

RALPH. All right . . .

BRYAN. 'Course it has. Copper takes a bribe it weakens the whole case, dunnit? Stands to reason. The whole case against us is rendered suspect.

RALPH. We're guilty as charged, man.

BRYAN. Yeah, I ain't saying—I'm just saying when the Court of Law is dealing with scumbags like him they can't be relied upon, quite frankly. I mean, an English court would have slung it out, wouldn't they? There ain't nothing dodgier than a bent copper.

RALPH. Yeah.

BRYAN. 'Course I ain't saying I'm *innocent*—I just ain't as guilty as you, that's all.

RALPH. What difference does it make?

BRYAN. That fucking lawyer, she said she'd look for loopholes and that—what was that if it weren't a loophole? Bent coppers supplying the information. In England they'd've chucked it out and we'd be down the boozer now.

RALPH. I doubt it.

BRYAN. 'Course we fucking would. Bent copper there's no case.

RALPH. It's not 'bent'; they take it for granted everyone's working a scam . . .

BRYAN. Yeah but that ain't . . .

RALPH. The Customs found us with it in our fucking Y-fronts, man—now smarten up.

BRYAN. I know they did; I ain't contesting that. That ain't contested. But what I'm saying is—who tipped 'em off? Number one cunt.

RALPH. All right.

BRYAN. I mean don't try to tell me they're gonna hang us on that 'cos it just don't stand up. For fuck's sake, how can it? I mean fair's fair, ennit? It's not as though we fucking killed anybody, is it? I mean who did we kill? It's just not realistic. It isn't a realistic sentence to pass. I mean why not hanging for pinching a loaf of bread or poking your best mate's missis or something? It's prehistoric. I'll take what I got coming, but no way can you tell me hanging is appropriate for a thing like this. It's just not playing the fucking game. Oi—is it?

RALPH. No it's not a game.

BRYAN. That's what I'm saying. I couldn't believe it when that cunt read that out. Hanged by the neck until you are dead. Jesus. Who'd he think he's talking to? Fucking multiple murderer or something? Who'd I fucking kill? I hate killers; I think they should be hanged. But I ain't one. It doesn't describe me at all. I'm not even fucking 21. They knew that, didn't they? I mean that was pointed out to them, wasn't it? That I'm under age?

RALPH. Yeah.

BRYAN. Well there ought to be a fucking law against it.

RALPH. There is a law and you got on the wrong end of it.

BRYAN. You an' all. Don't try and tell me you ain't gonna get the same. That's the only satisfaction I've received so far.

RALPH. Why don't you just shut up about the law. If the law's an ass you're the shit that comes out of it.

BRYAN. No I'm saying an international law—there's got to be an international law, respected by all nations alike, which it's a crime to hang an under-aged person for this. Anyway they can't hang a fucking Englishman.

RALPH. Yeah well that's just what they can do.

BRYAN. What—foreigners hang an Englishman? Leave it out; it's a complete contradiction in terms. I mean who gave 'em their fucking legal system in the first place . . .

RALPH. Oh man . . .

BRYAN. No, go on—who give it to 'em? We did. Fucking muggins as usual—we give 'em everything then they go and turn on us.

RALPH. You know, in certain circumstances I suppose you could be quite entertaining . . .

BRYAN. I'd been all right if it hadn't been for you. Why didn't you fucking leave me alone? Heroin? I never touched the stuff back home. I hate fucking pushers; they should all be shoved down the lavatory . . . What you laughing at now, you cunt? You're always laughing at something. You done that in court, I seen you. No wonder they was indisposed against us, what with you smirking like that all the bleedin' time . . .

RALPH. Maybe I find the whole thing funny.

BRYAN. Oh yeah fucking hilarious. Got me in stitches here. I expect you'll be laughing when they put that rope round your neck an' all.
    Oh I don't wanna think about it. Gives me the fucking creeps. And another thing: that fucking accent of yours. I could see they hated you the moment you opened your mouth. What you trying to be—Clint Eastwood or something? You an Englishman or not?

RALPH. Yeah I'm English.

BRYAN. Well why don't you fucking talk like one?

RALPH. I've done a lot of travelling, Bryan.

BRYAN. Well I wish you fucking hadn't. I wish you'd stayed home and sat in front of the telly, instead of . . . Why the fuck couldn't you have left me alone? I was all right.

RALPH. Oh yeah!

BRYAN. I was.

RALPH. Yeah, you were wonderful.

BRYAN. I ain't saying I was wonderful; I'm saying I was all right.
I didn't need . . .

RALPH. You needed the money! Well, you *wanted* it. Quit telling
yourself lies, why don't you? You did it for the bread. 25,000
and a first-class flight on to Australia—you couldn't resist it.
A fortnight in Oz then back home like the fucking Sugar
Plum Fairy—Look Ma! You're a victim of your own greed.
The new English disease, or haven't you heard . . ?

BRYAN. Bollocks . . .

RALPH. . . . That's why you were perfect. Or we *thought* you were
perfect.

BRYAN. I wasn't perfect, was I?

RALPH. You were not. You were a complete asshole.

BRYAN. You're lucky I haven't broken your fucking neck for you
by now.

RALPH. I am?

BRYAN. Fucking lucky. I tell you, they shouldn't've put us in the
same cell together 'cos I'm gonna do for you.

RALPH. Yeah well I sleep with one eye open.

BRYAN. You fucking would.

RALPH. Because that's the only way you'd do it, pal . . .

BRYAN. Stop calling me pal; I ain't your pal . . .

RALPH. You're all talk, like all the English these days . . .

BRYAN. You don't half fucking know a lot about the English
considering you don't live there no more . . .

RALPH. . . . They're gonna hang you by the neck until you're
fucking dead and then you'll be number one jerk.

BRYAN. Yeah well they're gonna hang you too mate so you're not
so bloody smart, are you?

RALPH. You should've gone to Margate for your holidays.

BRYAN. I nearly did. You don't know how true you spoke—I
  nearly did! 'Cept I won this fucking trip in a raffle. (*Laughs.*)
  Fucking laugh, ennit? That's your sort of humour, ennit?
  Cunt wins a foreign holiday in a raffle, ends up getting
  himself topped. You like all that, don't you?

RALPH (*seriously*). Yeah that's pretty damned funny.

BRYAN. Cunt. I ain't even been abroad before! Har har har!

  The GAOLER *passes by. He's a large Sikh.*

GAOLER. All right boys?

BRYAN. Fuck off, you different-coloured bastard.

RALPH. Careful.

GAOLER. Going home soon Bryan. (*He passes on.*)

BRYAN. What you mean 'careful'. You mean I might get into
  trouble?

RALPH. I mean he might come back and knock seven different
  kinds of shit out of you.

BRYAN. Hilarious. What is this country anyway? They got Chinks
  everywhere and they got fucking Pakis running the gaols.
  Sounds like a pretty fucked-up sort of place to me.

RALPH. Sounds just like home.

BRYAN. What d'*you* know?

RALPH. He's not a Paki.

BRYAN. Well whatever he is.

RALPH. How could he be a Paki?

BRYAN. What are you gonna tell me—he's a fucking Jap or
  something?

RALPH. He's a Sikh. And it's *not* a surprise to see him here.
  Wherever you go in the world you find Sikhs in jobs like
  this—they have a reputation for toughness . . .

BRYAN (*suddenly*). Oh fucking hell though, it ain't fair!

  He buries his head in his hands.
  RALPH *is wearing a Sony Walkman; he pulls the headphones over his
  ears and listens to the music.*

BRYAN. Don't put that on! Come on, take it off.

RALPH. Why?

BRYAN. I don't know.

> RALPH *looks at him for a while then takes it off again. Long silence.*

BRYAN. I mean you're carrying on as though this sort of thing is happening to you all the time. I mean don't pretend you couldn't give a stuff, all right? You gotta be as chewed up about it as I am, haven't you? Unless you want to fucking die, which I doubt.

> RALPH *says nothing. They look at one another.*

RALPH. Just don't you think of coming up on me when I'm asleep . . .

BRYAN. No, no, no . . .

RALPH. I mean it—don't even think of it.

BRYAN. All right, no need to threaten me.

RALPH. I just want to make it clear to you, OK?

BRYAN. It's clear, it's clear. Fucking hell, touchy entcha?

RALPH. Yeah. I don't like people coming up on me.

BRYAN. Well you're in the wrong place, son.

> RALPH *looks at him.*

—In here. This is the wrong place for you.

RALPH. Just leave me alone.

BRYAN. Yeah I'll leave you alone. Just like you left me alone.

RALPH. I'm sorry . . .

BRYAN. Oh fucking hell, he's apologising!

RALPH. . . . But you shouldn't win prizes.

> RALPH *laughs at him—a curious, joyless laugh. It's creepy.*

Scene Two

Hotel, Penang.
It is a large, adequately furnished, impersonal hotel room with one or two ethnic touches to distinguish it from other hotel rooms in other parts of the world.
GEORGE and WENDY come in—BRYAN's parents. They are both in their forties, although they both have the worried and hunched bearing of people older than their age. With them is LILLY, BRYAN's sister. She is about 19—overweight, sluttish, glazed. She carries a very small baby, invariably crying its head off. They have all just arrived after a long flight. Leading the way is the female LAWYER who is handling BRYAN's case—Mrs Mahalingam. She is a crisp, well-turned out woman in her thirties or younger. She is an elegant Tamil, speaks excellent English.
WENDY and LILLY both have loud, uncompromising voices; GEORGE is very quiet.

LAWYER. Ah yes, this is it; I think they made a little mistake downstairs, actually.

GEORGE. Yes, I think so.

LAWYER. But I think it's quite clean and comfortable; we've used it before many times . . .

GEORGE. Thank you.

LAWYER. I think you'll be OK here.

GEORGE. Very nice thank you—and thank you for coming all the way out to the airport. I did run a check and I had a reasonable idea of the route in, didn't I Wendy?

LAWYER. Oh it is no problem.

GEORGE. Not that we know where we are, do we Wendy? (*Laughs—a throaty, smoker's laugh.*) Never been to this part of the world before, to tell you the . . .

LAWYER. Well you are in Penang island proper; it is separated from the mainland by a short stretch of water with very regular ferries. The city here is known as Georgetown.

GEORGE. Really? Well that's suitable isn't it 'cos George is my name, see. George in Georgetown. Don't suppose there'll be many Georges as such here, will there? They'll have their own names, won't they? Why is that? Because the British was here—is it?

LAWYER. Yes they were here, very much so.

GEORGE. I thought so. 'Cos there are a lot of Georgetowns all over the world, aren't there? Jamestowns. Victorias. It's funny how they hang on to those old names after all this time, isn't it? You'd think they'd want to change 'em, you know, sort of get their own names.

The baby is crying.

WENDY. I think he wants a feed Lil.

LILLY. I know he does.

WENDY. I'm just telling you because sometimes you don't seem to realise . . .

LILLY. 'Course I realise—whose baby is it—yours or mine?

WENDY. It ain't mine!

LILLY. No.

WENDY. I finished with all that, girl, bloody ages ago, thank Christ . . .

LILLY. Well then.

LAWYER. Now apparently this is a suite . . .

GEORGE. Yes they told us it was a suite . . .

LAWYER. . . . So your room should be through here . . . Yes.

LILLY. Right.

The LAWYER *goes ahead to check the adjoining room.*

GEORGE. Try and say thank you, Lil, because she's been very kind to us.

LILLY. Shut up, you fucking crawler.

LILLY goes with the baby into the next room. GEORGE *and* WENDY *are together.*

GEORGE. Well it seems to have everything, dunnit? (*He checks something.*) What's this?

WENDY. What you bloody talking, Georgetown?

GEORGE. I'm just being 'amickable' with her, aren't I? She's Bry's lawyer—stands to reason we should get on with her.

WENDY. 'Georgetown—my name's George'—she'll think you're mad. Leave that case; you won't know where to put nothing.

GEORGE. Oh I'm bleedin' tired though, Wend. You reckon it's that jet-lag thing I got?

WENDY. I dunno what you got mate, but whatever it is it ain't worth having.

GEORGE. What is she, d'you reckon? Only I always thought Malayans was a darker race.

WENDY. Don't rumple all them things up.

GEORGE. No, I'm just . . .

WENDY. Just don't rumple 'em. They're packed so I know where everything is.

GEORGE. No I'm just . . .

WENDY. What you looking for?

GEORGE. Umm . . .

WENDY. Come on, get out of it. You're worse than her and that kid.

GEORGE. I thought I'd put me sandals on, only with this tropical climate . . .

WENDY. I'll find 'em for you in a minute. Sit down there. God, I haven't had a decent smoke since we left home. (*Lights up.*) Trust you to get us in a no-smoking area on the plane . . .

GEORGE. Well I thought with Lil's kiddie—you know, passive smoking. I was reading about that in the *Sunday Times* . . .

WENDY. You consider me for a change. (*Coughs grotesquely.*) God I needed that. 'Passive smoking!' Stupid bastard.

GEORGE. It was a very interesting drive in, I thought. It's still too early to form a view, sort of thing, but from what I could see—most of the residents appeared to be Chinese. I always thought Malayans were a dark race, somewhat like the Indians. Darker than the Pakis. It's terrible when you come to think of it though, Wend, what you don't know about the geography of the world we live in.

WENDY. I dunno what fucking world you live in; it ain't the same as mine, I'll tell you.

GEORGE. No, I was just trying to place the Malayans . . .

WENDY. Place 'em in the sea, I would.
    The bastards.

GEORGE. Well we'll see, won't we?

WENDY. *Seen* already, haven't we?

> *They sit staring into space for a while.* GEORGE *lights up. He has a coughing fit too.*
> *Followed by more silence.*
> *At last the* LAWYER *returns.*

LAWYER. Well your daughter seems to be all right in there.

GEORGE. Yes, lovely, thank you.

LAWYER. You don't seem to have much of a view, I'm afraid . . .

GEORGE. No, I was thinking . . .

WENDY (*stonily*). We don't really want a view thank you.

LAWYER. No.

GEORGE. So, you'll appreciate we're both very interested to
    know how Bryan is. I mean when you last saw him and . . .

LAWYER. Well obviously he's very upset . . .

GEORGE. Yes.

LAWYER. . . . And a little bitter. I think it's hard for him to take
    in at the present time . . .

GEORGE. Well it would be hard for anybody, no matter what
    he's . . .

LAWYER. But as I told you in the car we have not given up hope.
    Not by any means.

GEORGE. Thank you. Well that's good to hear isn't it Wendy?

    WENDY *says nothing.*

    —So what hope can there actually be, would you say? At this
    moment in time.

LAWYER. Well, regarding *Bryan*, let me say—in Bryan's case as
    distinct from Ralph's—a pardon on appeal is an altogether
    more feasible prospect. I don't want to raise false hopes, not
    at all, but I think I can say that. I think that in Court we were

able to prove that the nature of their responsibility was quite different. Bryan was duped, there's agreement on that. Ralph is unmistakably the guilty one—he's a member of an international syndicate and all that . . .

GEORGE. Is he really? Tsk tsk tsk!

LAWYER. But Bryan was different, of course: first offence; not a user or supplier; just a tourist and a dupe on this one single occasion. Also, there is the question of his I.Q. rating. His I.Q. being—um—so low, he is the type who is more easily led astray. We were able to prove that in this sense he was led astray. Courts in this part of the world set great store by this sort of evidence, you know . . .

GEORGE. Do they, yes—well if you think it will be a helpful, a chink of light sort of thing . . .

LAWYER. Well I'm reasonably optimistic about this whole area of our appeal, frankly. It is more likely to be taken notice of on appeal than in Court, oddly enough.

GEORGE. Yes, I see.

WENDY. Sorry, you say his I.Q. is what? Very low, you say?

LAWYER. Well . . .

WENDY. You see I don't know what you mean by that at all.

GEORGE. Well it's his I.Q. isn't it?

LAWYER. Well we were able to produce a renowned psychiatrist, you know, who was able to measure it. It's not *chronically* low—please don't get me wrong . . .

GEORGE. No no, you have to . . .

WENDY. You mean he's not very bright. That's what you're trying to say, isn't it?

GEORGE. No, listen Wend . . .

WENDY. A psychiatrist? Excuse me but I got to laugh, quite frankly . . .

LAWYER. Compared to Ralph certainly—there is a discernible gap. That is the crucial factor. Only I.Q.-wise, you understand. There is definitely a question of leader and led.

GEORGE. Yeah that's what it is, see, Wend. The other boy—what it is with him—well, he's clever, isn't he?

LAWYER. Well he does have a very high rating . . .

WENDY. Oh he's clever.

LAWYER. Anyhow, this is one line we will certainly be taking and frankly I believe we should be grasping at every straw.

GEORGE. Thank you.

WENDY. Yes well that's what it is, isn't it? Grasping at straws.

GEORGE. Well it's a question of you've got to take every . . .

LAWYER. The law here is very strong on this matter.

WENDY. Yeah well we have heard, thank you.

GEORGE. Yes we—have heard.

LAWYER. Personally, although the situation is very serious, I believe there are grounds for optimism.

GEORGE. Thank you very much.

WENDY. But it's not your boy, is it?

GEORGE. No, listen to the lady, Wend . . .

WENDY. So I don't know what you mean you're 'optimistic'. I mean it's me that's optimistic or pessimistic, isn't it? I mean I'm the one who's involved, you know what I mean?

LAWYER (*kindly*). Yes I know.

WENDY. I mean I know you're probably doing the best you can and you're probably quite a sincere person but you see I'm not going to just stand by and let that boy hang, am I? I haven't come all the way out here to attend a hanging.

GEORGE. I don't think we actually attend . . .

WENDY. I've been in touch with my MP. He's a leading Labour MP and he's taken an interest in our case . . .

GEORGE. He's very good.

WENDY. He's written letters and made deputations to this that and the other . . .

GEORGE. We live in an inner-city area, you know.

WENDY. And it's a *personal* interest he's taken, not just so he can get votes . . .

GEORGE. He doesn't have to do it; he's already an MP.

WENDY. At this moment he's trying to raise the issue with the Queen.

GEORGE. It's funny, we never went to church at all before this happened. (*Laughs and coughs.*)

WENDY. The Prime Minister is expected to intervene.

LAWYER. Of course, all that is to the good.

GEORGE. The Prime Minister does usually intervene, isn't that right? As a last resort, sort of thing?

Pause. They ponder this.

—I expect there'll be some sort of deal going on right now, at top level, sort of thing, won't there? You just don't know, do you?

LAWYER. Well I'll telephone you later—I'd better let you get settled in now.

GEORGE. Yes, thank you.

LAWYER. If there's anything you want to know, anything at all— please don't hesitate to ring me at the office or at home.

GEORGE. Oh thank you . . . Oh I see your home address is on the back. That's useful, isn't it? Cor that's a long name, isn't it?

LAWYER. Mrs Mahalingam. But you can call me Katie if you like—everyone calls me that. It's the nearest thing.

GEORGE. What is it, a Malayan name is it?

LAWYER. No it's a Tamil name actually.

GEORGE. Oh.

LAWYER. India, you know.

GEORGE. Oh! Oh I was wondering what you—I was just saying, wasn't I Wend?

LAWYER. Yes we're simply all over the place.

GEORGE. You're telling me. I mean where we come from . . .

WENDY. Thank you—we'll be in touch.

The LAWYER *goes.*
GEORGE *reads the card.*

GEORGE. Mrs Maha ... Mahal ... I can't even say it, Wend!

WENDY. 'We live in an inner-city area'. You pratt.

GEORGE. What about it?

WENDY. You berk.

GEORGE. Well we do.

WENDY. What's it got to do with anything?

GEORGE. Well, she's an Indian. She'll know we sort of live amongst 'em. Other Indians and Pakis and that. Which we *do* live amongst 'em.

WENDY. You'd send 'em all back home if you had your way.

GEORGE. I wouldn't! When did I say that? I ain't never said nothing like that. I might have in jest once or twice. You're talking about in jest.

WENDY. All right. Shut up.

GEORGE. I don't think it can do any harm to tell her that we move amongst her kind.

WENDY. Jesus Christ.

GEORGE. But I do think it's very enlightened of them, though Wend, to have an Indian as a lawyer. Because they're not in the majority here. If they was it would be India, wouldn't it? It wouldn't be Malaya at all. Plus the fact she's a woman. How many lawyers are there in England that are Indian *and* women? It would be interesting to know that, Wend. It's funny, ennit? You go abroad and you come across little things like that that really surprise you, you know what I mean? They sort of ... (*mimes surprise*). Don't you think that's enlightened?

WENDY. You can't help being enlightened; your head's full of holes.

GEORGE (*laughs good-naturedly*). That's good Wend.

WENDY. We haven't come here to be enlightened or observe the various what's'isnames—we come here because our boy's being hanged! Or has it escaped your attention?

GEORGE. I know; I suppose I'm just sort of seeking a refuge really.

WENDY. Well don't seek it in stupidity, if you can help it. We got to keep a clear head or they'll treat us like scum. They're just like at home, only worse.

GEORGE. No, I'm just saying . . .

WENDY. Well don't say. Don't say nothing. I'm fed up with the sound of your voice. I'm not taking my son home in a box.

GEORGE. Can you get my pills out of there, because . . .

WENDY. Here.

GEORGE. Ta. Got the bleedin' shakes already, I have. Which ones is it—I can't see without me glasses . . . Where's me glasses . . ? Tell you something else, though, Wend; that girl didn't ought to talk like that to me in front of other people. Did you hear what she said to me? I dunno—ever since she got herself pregnant—her whole manner seems to have altered with me. The things she says. No one's ever spoken to me the way she does. Except you, but that's normal. I got to have respect, though, Wend—I think I've got to have a word with her. No way can she talk like that to me, specially not in front of strangers.

WENDY. She didn't hear.

GEORGE. I think she did. D'you think she didn't? She probably didn't. But still.

WENDY. I don't know where your bloody glasses are. Have I got to think of everything?

GEORGE. No, it's just these labels, they make 'em so small . . .

WENDY. These are your carba . . . carba . . .

GEORGE. Carbamazepine! That's the ones.

WENDY. What a fucking hole, though! Did you see it on the way in?

GEORGE. Yeah I thought it was . . .

WENDY. Bloody shanty-town full of Chinese and they're gonna hang our Bryan. They got a fucking cheek.
Oi Lil!

LILLY *comes in* (*without her baby*).

LILLY. What?

WENDY. What you bring this for? (*She holds up a swimming costume that she's unpacking from the case.*)

LILLY. What d'you think?

WENDY. You can forget going swimming here, all right?

LILLY. Why not?

WENDY. 'Cos you're not, that's all.

LILLY. They got the sea haven't they?

WENDY. They may have the sea BUT YOU AIN'T GOING IN IT!

GEORGE. Shh! Shh!

LILLY (*laughs*). That's that prickly heat you got there.

WENDY. FANCY BRINGING THIS, YOU COW!

LILLY. WHO YOU CALLING A COW?

GEORGE. Shh, come on now . . .

LILLY. It's supposed to be the fucking tropics!

GEORGE. Well it *is* the tropics, Wend—fair enough. There was a lot of them palm trees on the way in.

WENDY. We are here because our Bryan—your brother—has been sentenced to death by a bunch of savages. Can you get that into your thick skull? You an' all. How d'you think it would look in the papers if there was this picture of you swanning about in the water while our Bryan's on death row? They'd love that, wouldn't they?

LILLY. All right—I wasn't going to go now—I was going to leave it until after.

Pause. LILLY realises what she's said.

—Fuck it.

GEORGE. I suppose they would print a picture like that, really. I suppose we ought to be on our guard, sort of thing. I hadn't thought of that. I suppose we're newsworthy really, aren't we?

WENDY. You always fucking have been.
We got to be serious about this, all of us, or they're gonna hang our Bryan. (*Throws the costume back.*) It won't fit you no more anyway.

LILLY. Nothing does fit me. When am I gonna get my figure back?

WENDY. Shouldn't drink so much, should you?

LILLY. Look who's talking!

WENDY. I am.

LILLY. Yeah, look who's talking!

GEORGE. Don't start rowing—my nerves won't stand it.

LILLY. They won't hang him; they wouldn't fucking dare.

WENDY. Better hope you're right, girl.

GEORGE. Er, Lil—just a . . . before we er . . .

LILLY. What?

GEORGE. No it's just . . .

LILLY. What's the matter with him?

WENDY. You've upset him.

LILLY. Do what?

WENDY. Why don't you mind how you talk to your father?

LILLY. Ooh, my 'father'!

WENDY. Don't put your feet on that; I don't want them complaining about muddy marks.

GEORGE. No, what it is, Lilly—I'll be quite honest with you . . .

LILLY. Oh that'll make a change.

GEORGE. What it is . . .

LILLY. You already said that.

GEORGE. When that woman was here you had a little go at me, didn't you? It's all right—we're all under pressure, and I expect a little niggle or two will be coming out in the ensuing days. But, well, what it is, you see Lilly—a family, it's like the insides of a car, you know? Every bit under there depends on every other bit; they can't function if one bit isn't turning over and doing its proper job an' that. That's what a family's like, see? You get one that's out of tune—or 'synch' as they call it—well, you've a breakdown, haven't you? Chaos. You have to pull over on to the hard shoulder. You get what I mean? The hard shoulder of life. I mean I don't blame you—don't get me wrong; we're all under pressure. I'll let it go with a word this time, but I'd really rather you didn't address me like you did just now in front of Mrs Marlgam.

LILLY. What d'you know about the insides of a car? I haven't finished that feed yet . . . (*Going.*) I feel like a fucking cow, don't I?

She goes back to her room.

WENDY. She's grown up very fast, that girl.

GEORGE. I don't know. She defies her parents.

WENDY. Haven't you taken that pill yet?

GEORGE. You think it's all right to drink the water? Better not, eh? I should've asked Mrs Marlgam.

WENDY. Don't be stupid.

GEORGE. What?

WENDY. You don't want to get ill, do you? Which you will get ill if you drink the water. Don't give 'em the satisfaction. Use the Coke we brought.

GEORGE. Oh yeah. (*He goes to bathroom with large bottle of Coca-Cola.*)

WENDY (*stubbing out cigarette*). Got to think of everything round here.

Scene Three

The prison cell.
RALPH *and the* **GAOLER** *are playing chess.* **BRYAN** *is absent.*
RALPH *has his headset on; his foot is slowly keeping beat. He and the* **GAOLER** *are smoking marijuana—passing the joint to and fro. There is still the soft clamour from the other rooms—but there is a cool, laid-back atmosphere.*
The **GAOLER** *has to summon enormous resources of concentration to play.*
RALPH *takes down his headset.*

RALPH. Wait a minute—you're moving your king into check.

GAOLER. Pardon?

RALPH. Your king. You're in check there from my bishop. See?

GAOLER. Oh. Never mind.

RALPH. What d'you mean never mind? You can't move your king into check.

GAOLER. I will move him away next time.

RALPH. Are you sure you've played this game before?

GAOLER. Oh yes—I am the champion round here.

RALPH. I'd like to meet the opposition.

GAOLER. I play Punjabi rules.

RALPH. Even in Punjab you can't move your king into check.

GAOLER. Maybe.

RALPH. Definitely.

GAOLER. You're too good for me, Ralph. Here—it has gone out . . .

RALPH. Thanks . . .

GAOLER. Your hand is not shaking at all.

RALPH. No.

GAOLER. The other one, Bryan—he is going all to pieces.

RALPH. He's young.

GAOLER. That has nothing to do with it, believe me. I have seen big men—tough, you know—(*mimes 'goes to pieces'*). He got you caught.

RALPH *shrugs*.

—He is a racist.

RALPH. He hasn't had time to become anything else.

GAOLER. But here everything is forgiven. Here you can say anything. You know why I am good at my job?

RALPH. Because you're a big hairy sadistic bastard.

GAOLER (*laughs*). No! Well, maybe, a little. But no, I am good at my job because I am indifferent on the question of abuse.

Really, it is all water off the duck's back. You can only do
your work properly and well if you are indifferent.

RALPH. Yes.
You know, when it comes to the moment—I expect to have
no feeling whatsoever. Just as I've never had any feeling
about any person. Not for the people whose lives I've ruined.
They *say* I've ruined.

GAOLER. Well we give you a drug, you know—to deaden the
feelings.

RALPH. I won't need it.

GAOLER. It is not compulsory. We can get you some cocaine, if
you like.

RALPH (*amused*). Really?

GAOLER. Yes, just be sure to place your order, in good time.

RALPH. So you'll smuggle it in?

GAOLER. Yes. In here. (*Taps his turban.*) Better than the
underpants!

RALPH. I'd like to see that, but I don't think I'll even need that.

GAOLER. Oh you will panic like anything when it comes to it.
They all do.

Scene Four

The prison visiting room.
BRYAN *is the only prisoner being visited. He is there opposite* WENDY,
GEORGE *and* LILLY (*with baby*). BRYAN *is chained at the wrists. A*
GAOLER *sits close by.*

WENDY. I'm very, very upset about this, though, Bryan, I am
really.

BRYAN. Well I ain't exactly over the moon about it, am I?

WENDY. Soon as you won that bleedin' prize I knew there'd be
trouble, didn't I George?

GEORGE. Well . . .

WENDY. And look at your hair—what have they done to it?

BRYAN. Never mind that. You spoken to a lawyer or not?

WENDY. Yeah she came out to the airport, didn't she?

GEORGE. Mrs Marlgam . . .

BRYAN. I don't mean her. For fuck's sake, she couldn't get you off a parking fine. I mean a proper English lawyer.

WENDY. Well in England, yeah—didn't we George?

GEORGE. Oh yeah, we . . .

BRYAN. What did he say?

WENDY. Well he said—but it's the MP really that we hold out the most hope for isn't it George?

GEORGE. What, Chris?

WENDY. Yeah.

GEORGE (to BRYAN). I call him Chris, like, because he said we ought to, didn't he? He's not a bit like an MP—he's . . .

BRYAN. What did he say?

GEORGE. Well he's very interested . . .

BRYAN. Interested! I'm 'interested' but there's fuck-all I can do about anything.

WENDY. He might even come out here but for the moment he's trying to raise it in the House of Parliament.

GEORGE. Yeah it's a sort of special what's'isname—privilege or something whereby he can raise it in the House. What's it called, a filibuster or something . . .

WENDY. Something like that.

GEORGE. I got a book on it indoors . . .

BRYAN. Book! You ain't got a fucking book on what I got in here. You ain't got a bloody video on it neither. Midnight Express? This is ten times as bad.

WENDY. The bastards.

GEORGE. I think perhaps you'd better keep your voice down, Bry.

BRYAN. Yeah? What they gonna do? Fine me? Give me an 'undred lines?

WENDY. He's got to shout, hasn't he? Let off steam a bit.

GEORGE. Yeah I know, but . . . I dunno.

BRYAN. You should see the poxy food they got in here. Fucking pig-swill, 'cept they wouldn't give it to pigs. I've had the running-shits ever since I come in here.

GEORGE. Oh, that's no joke that isn't.

BRYAN. What you gonna do for me then? Eh?

WENDY. We're going to get you out of here, Bryan . . .

BRYAN. 'Cos they can't carry this out, can they? It's outrageous. Tell 'em this: number one—I'm a minor; I ain't 21. Number two—I was led astray by a fucking syndicate on threat of my life. Number three—I'm English. Number four—they didn't ought to hang people for this sort of crime. I don't think that Paki tart got all that across, specially about being led astray on fear of my life an' that. Hanging! I couldn't believe my fucking ears. I thought they was having me on.

GEORGE. It could be they was just trying to scare you, Bry.

BRYAN. Well they fucking succeeded.

GEORGE. It could be that, couldn't it Wend?

WENDY. I'm so upset I don't know what to think.

GEORGE. See, it could be they proceed as though they got every intention of carrying out the what's'isname, the sentence, then at the last minute they say 'All right, we let you off'.

BRYAN. Yeah. You reckon?

GEORGE. They used to do that. It's in history, you know. Chris reckons it's a possibility, don't he Wend?

BRYAN. What, he said that, did he?

GEORGE. Yeah. Well, it was sort of off the record, like. He can't make that sort of information public, can he?

BRYAN. Only it's completely outrageous. I ain't hardly done nothing.

GEORGE. No. Well it was heroin, Bryan.

WENDY. Oh shut up George.

BRYAN. I know it was fucking heroin.

GEORGE. No, I'm just saying—if we're going to help him we've got to face the facts. That's all I'm saying.

BRYAN. I know it was fucking heroin!

GEORGE. All right—shh!

BRYAN. But it was only twelve ounces.

GEORGE. No, it's just that I saw this programme—d'you remember watching it, Wend?

BRYAN. Very nice for you.

GEORGE. No but some of the things they showed about the results of heroin and that. I mean it wasn't sensationalised—it was quite educational really. God, they got these little kids with . . .

WENDY. Shut up.

BRYAN. Give it a fucking rest.

They all sit there lost in their thoughts for some time.

BRYAN (*To* LILLY). All right?

LILLY. No so bad.

BRYAN. How's the baby then?

LILLY. He's all right.

BRYAN. Where's Gary?

LILLY. Dunno. Don't care neither.

BRYAN. What, it's all over is it?

LILLY *shrugs.*

—Good riddance, eh?

GEORGE. Oh, have you mentioned the papers?

WENDY. How could I have when you been with me all the time?

GEORGE. No, I thought you might have . . .

WENDY. You been here with me—you heard every word I said.

GEORGE. Suppose I have. (*Laughs and coughs.*)

BRYAN. What papers?

WENDY. We'll talk about it another time . . .

BRYAN. Talk about it now.

LILLY. They sold their story to the Sunday papers.

WENDY. Do you mind?

LILLY. No.

BRYAN. What story?

WENDY. Do-you-mind?

LILLY. No.

BRYAN. What story?

WENDY. Thank you very much.

LILLY. 'S all right.

WENDY. Go and tell the whole place—go on.

LILLY. It was him that brought it up.

BRYAN. Shut up. What story?

GEORGE. Well it's the story of—everything really . . .

BRYAN. What story you got? You ain't got a fucking story.

GEORGE. Well what it is really, Bry—it's a sort a hin-depth
account—more of an account than a story—about you as a
child and young man an' that . . .

BRYAN. Oh charming.

GEORGE. I think it will be quite sensitively handled on the whole
really.

BRYAN. I bet you do. How much they giving you for that?

GEORGE. Well a final figure has yet to be . . .

LILLY. £10,000.

BRYAN. Fucking hell.

WENDY. Would you go and wait outside please?

LILLY. No.

BRYAN. You done all right for yourselves ain't you? Considering you haven't got a story. I'm the one with the story, not you. Childhood? Mine only lasted ten minutes.

GEORGE. We appreciate everything you say Bryan, but if you could just keep your voice down . . .

BRYAN. Ah yeah but I'll be dead, won't I? So I can't *tell* my story! Fucking tasty—I thought you was coming out here to help me, turns out it's so you can sell your story.

GEORGE. We couldn't have come without it, Bry.

BRYAN. Fucking tasty. Proper cunt I'm going to look, aren't I, swinging at the end of a rope and you lot poncing off to Spain. I suppose it won't happen if I get off, will it?

GEORGE. Oh yeah. Won't it Wend? We checked that, didn't we, and they told us there was that clause.

WENDY. Shut your mouth.

GEORGE. You got to be realistic, Bryan . . .

BRYAN. Oh don't worry about that; I'm realistic in here. It's getting realer every day.

GEORGE. No, how d'you think we could of afforded it, coming out here?

BRYAN. I thought the Government paid.

GEORGE. No, Bryan—the paper paid. What's the harm in that?

BRYAN. What's the harm? I'll tell you what's the harm . . . If you don't know I can't tell you. Only I hope you'll have the decency to let the body get cold before it comes out.

   WENDY *has started to cry.*

GEORGE. It's all right Wend—it's just family talk.
   Ennit Bry?

BRYAN. Family talk? (*He scoffs.*) No such thing, is there? All fucking grunts, ennit?
   Come on—don't cry; they enjoy it when you start that in here. Think they've won, don't they?

WENDY. I'm very, very upset about it all.

LILLY. You already said that.

WENDY. Seeing you in here. Christ almighty.

GEORGE. We did leave you some personal effects at the desk. I didn't know what the position was regarding them, so . . .

BRYAN. What did you bring?

GEORGE. Brought you some fags, toothpaste, biscuits, some soap. Brought you some magazines. Anything else, you just let us know, all right? I expect we're allowed to bring in food really.

BRYAN (*To* WENDY). Shut up, will you? Fucking depressing, having someone crying all the time. (*To* GEORGE.) Toilet paper.

GEORGE. Toilet paper? Yeah all right, Bry, toilet paper. Yeah, come on Wend—chin up, eh? We got to be positive, haven't we Bry?

BRYAN. Yeah.

GEORGE. The Arsenal's winning anyway. That new bloke's fitting in all right. He does some clever things, but I still think they was wrong to sell Charlie . . .

BRYAN. Oh fuck off!

He suddenly gets up and goes. The GAOLER *looks confused but follows.*

WENDY. Bryan! You come back here and say goodbye! Bryan!

He sticks his head round the door. He doesn't look at them, but raises a hand.

BRYAN. Yeah, bye . . .

He goes.

WENDY. In chains.

GEORGE. Yeah. You don't think he has to have 'em on all the time, do you? I'll ask.

WENDY. Bloody chained up like an animal or something.

GEORGE. Yeah well, worse than an animal, isn't it?

WENDY. Bloody Arabs, they're all bloody barbarians. It's enough to turn you into a racialist. Come on, let's get out of here.

GEORGE. Yeah, come on . . .'

WENDY. Don't you ever let me cry like that again. I'm never going to cry again—d'you hear me? I didn't hardly see him.

She speaks to LILLY *in a new, harsh voice.*

—You comin' or you want them to keep you here an' all?

They go, followed by LILLY.

Scene Five

The prison cell.
BRYAN *is alone, lying on the bunk reading boxing magazines.*
The GAOLER *comes in.*

BRYAN. What?

GAOLER. I am to keep you company.

BRYAN. I don't want any company, do I?

GAOLER. How are you?

He sits down, intent upon staying.

BRYAN. Oh for fuck's sake. I got all them out there to talk to, haven't I?

GAOLER. They are other prisoners.

BRYAN. Yeah well I prefer other prisoners, all right?

GAOLER. They do not speak your language. Except for the German boy and he is elsewhere.

BRYAN. Yeah well . . .

GAOLER. It was not a very useful interview with your parents, I think?

BRYAN scoffs and says nothing.

—It is most upsetting when a family cannot sit down and speak with one another. I have seen something of this and have taken great care to make sure I always speak properly to my sons.

BRYAN. Well that's bully for you, ennit?
Look, I got all these magazines, haven't I? I'm quite happy— or I was till you come in here.

GAOLER. OK.

BRYAN. Thank you very much.

GAOLER. I must remember I am not social worker; I am only prison-guard.

BRYAN. Fucking hell, don't send a social worker in here; I got enough problems.

Pause. The GAOLER *doesn't go.*

—All right, tell you what: say if you had to bet, sort of thing. You know, if you had to bet your life on it . . . what would you say's gonna happen? Is this sentence gonna be carried out, d'you reckon?

GAOLER. You are asking me for hope.

BRYAN. No, no, I'm just asking you a straight question . . .

GAOLER. If I had to bet my life—I cannot imagine being in such an extreme situation as this; it is completely, er . . . hypothetical . . .

BRYAN. All right, forget it. Forget I asked, if you can't answer a simple straightforward question.

GAOLER. I think you should make your peace.

BRYAN. Right. See, you can answer. It's not difficult, is it? I see. You reckon, then?

GAOLER. I am saying you should make your peace in any case, regardless of what happens.

BRYAN. Yeah well that doesn't apply, does it? because I'm not religious.

GAOLER. I know.

BRYAN. You know that—you know everything, don't you?

GAOLER. Religion would be useful but not essential. I am not actually speaking about religion; I am speaking about you, within yourself. You have a golden opportunity, which very few of us ever get: you can achieve if you like a kind of greatness.

BRYAN. A kind of what? Greatness?

GAOLER. A greatness of spirit.

BRYAN. What, in here?

GAOLER. In here especially. Perhaps only.

BRYAN. They better start feeding us properly first.

GAOLER. Most people's lives, what are they? Nothing. They come and they go; they do not even disturb the ripples on the pond of the world. They are never tested. You have now the supreme test; it is happening to you now.

BRYAN. Is that a fact?

GAOLER. You should let . . .

BRYAN. Yeah well why don't we forget it, yeah?

GAOLER. . . . You should let your ego break free. Let it go where your body cannot.

BRYAN. OK, I give it up. D'you see it? It went out the window— you missed it! I'll give up smoking an' all.

GAOLER. Where I come from a boy of 12 has more spirituality than you.

BRYAN. Yeah? Well why didn't you fucking stay there. Pakis are always going on about 'Where I come from' and all that. Yet they can't wait to get away from their own bloody country, can they?

GAOLER. There is poison in your head—you should try to release it . . .

BRYAN. Oi—I'm a dangerous man, all right?
They reckon you're a hard man. 'Cos you're some special breed of Paki or something. You know what? I don't think you are at all. You don't look it to me—you certainly don't talk like it. You talk like a poof, if you really wanna know. Know what I mean, a poof, a faggot? You wanna be more careful, going into people's cells like this. I'm a dangerous prisoner.

GAOLER. Yes you have been a danger to society.

BRYAN. No, I am now. I still am—highly dangerous. Stands to reason, dunnit? Else why are they hanging me?

Pause.

—Fucking boring in here, I'll tell you.

Is that what you come in here for Mushtapha? Bit of
aggravation, was it? Stir up the prisoners?
Come on then.

GAOLER. What are you doing?

BRYAN. Come on, see who's best. It don't matter to me, does it?
Come on, you foreign fucker.

He smacks the GAOLER *round the face. He starts dancing round
him, moving like a boxer and smacking his face.*
He laughs with each blow. The blows get harder—they ring out. The
GAOLER *follows him and waits.*
At last BRYAN *lunges with a dangerous punch; the* GAOLER
*dodges it, gets behind him and pins both his arms. It is ridiculously
easy for him.*
BRYAN *cries out in pain.*

BRYAN. All right, all right . . . Take it easy . . .

The GAOLER *lets him go.*

—You broke my fucking arm; I heard a crack, you bastard.
That's fucking wrestling, that what you did. I was boxing.
Don't you know the difference? Why couldn't you stick to the
rules, once in a while?

GAOLER. Come on, it's OK. Shake.

BRYAN. Fuck off.

GAOLER. We'll shake later.
Hard man.

BRYAN. I was boxing! Anyone can bloody wrestle.

GAOLER. Ah well you are on the wrong side to make the rules,
Bryan.

BRYAN. I distinctly heard a crack . . . What wrong side? What you
talking about? Wrong side of what? The law, I suppose.

GAOLER. Not only that.

BRYAN. You gotta be the weirdest prison-guard ever, man.

GAOLER (*laughs*). Yes I am pretty weird, aren't I?

BRYAN. I could report you—I hope you realise that. Smoking
dope in here with prisoners.

GAOLER. Ah well then I would *definitely* break the rules.

BRYAN. Wouldn't make any difference to me, would it?

GAOLER. You would be surprised. Oh, standards must be falling quite dramatically if that is how Englishmen talk these days.

BRYAN. Bollocks fucking Englishmen. There ain't no such thing no more ever since we let your lot in.

RALPH *comes in. Perhaps he is still wearing his wrist-chains—in which case he is unchained now.*

BRYAN. What's the matter with you, shit-for-brains?

RALPH. Huh?

BRYAN. 'Huh!?' You look as though you seen a ghost.

RALPH *(spookily)*. Maybe that's just what I did see!

BRYAN. Shut up.

RALPH. I just received the official visit. My mother.

GAOLER. Ah very nice!

BRYAN. She upset, was she?

RALPH. Well my mother doesn't get upset. I mean she pretends to be. That's not the point. I'm just very honoured, that's all. We all are, most honoured.

He sits down.

GAOLER. Absolutely. This is most true. Our mothers are jewels of the sky, our number one asset in life.

RALPH *closes his eyes under the headset.*

BRYAN. Fucking funny farm, this is.

Scene Six

The hotel.
TONI*'s room. It is similar to* GEORGE *and* WENDY*'s.*
It is early evening. TONI *is* RALPH*'s mother, but she's in her early forties. She looks glamorous and has an even tan. She looks like a nouveau riche.*
At the start she is in bed.
Beside her, still asleep is a young Malay—actually the BARMAN *at the*

hotel—although this is not clear until he puts his clothes on. She checks her watch.

When she speaks it is with a Lancashire accent, but it has an affected drawl that she probably thinks is posh.

TONI. Oh God . . . Come on! Come on, wakey-wakey!
Yes—you. Come on, the bell tolls.

    BARMAN *wakes, mumbling.*

TONI. I know, yes, come on . . .

    BARMAN *asks something.*

TONI. Never mind that. Don't ruin this beautiful silence with
questions. You've got to go. Come on, love, be a good boy
and get yourself dressed.

    He gets out of bed. He is about 20 years younger than she is—a very desirable hunk. She admires him from the bed.

    —Mm, did you really cop that Toni? Not losing your touch,
are you?

BARMAN. Hm?

TONI. Nothing, love, come on—chop-chop.

BARMAN. Not chop-chop.

TONI. All right, scram, skadoodle, on your bike or in your
rickshaw, whatever it is. Oh you young boys—you're so hard
to get shot of. An older man would be so grateful he'd run
for it but you have to . . . Go on, get your hands out me hair.
Go on—get yourself dressed; I'm expecting someone.

BARMAN. Here?

TONI. Yes, of course here.

BARMAN. OK.

    He gets dressed. She watches him for a moment. By this time we realise he is an employee at the hotel—he puts on bow-tie and white jacket, etc.

BARMAN. See you again, yeah?

TONI. Again?

BARMAN. Yeah. Maybe later, OK?

TONI. Your way of asking, it's perfect rapture.

BARMAN. Sure.

TONI. Go on now and polish your buttons.

> *He is dressed by now.*

> —You're fast at getting dressed, aren't you? Had plenty of practice, I expect.
> Eh! Don't forget your tray.

BARMAN. Ah!

> *He picks up the tray. It still has some drinks on it.*

TONI. You can leave the drinks, love.

BARMAN. You had yours already.

TONI. I know, I'll take the others as well.

BARMAN. They are for Room 421.

TONI. I'll see they get them. Just put them down there.
Pop everything on the bill, will you love?

BARMAN. Bill?

TONI. It's all right; I'm just having you on, pet. Joking, you know.

BARMAN. Yeah, English women always kidding around.

TONI. We have to, love; it's a cry for help.

BARMAN. Cry for help, I come fast.

TONI. I know that, love. See you in the bar.

BARMAN. OK.

> *He stands for a moment and adjusts his hair—not because it's ruffled, but because he's vain. She smiles.*
> *There is a knock on the door.*

BARMAN. You want me hide in the closet?

TONI. Certainly not. Open the door.

> *He opens the door. The* LAWYER *is there.*

BARMAN. Hi, come on in!

LAWYER. Oh, is this . . .?

TONI. Hello Katie, come on; I was expecting you.
Thank you!

She raises her glass to the BARMAN, *who goes.*

TONI. Hello love, I just had to have a drink.

LAWYER. You're lucky, there have been all kinds of complaints
about the room service here.

TONI. Oh I haven't got any complaints, not yet.

LAWYER. So have you had some sleep?

TONI. Off and on, you know.

TONI *is out of the bed, beginning to get dressed. There is a pair of her
pants way over the other side of the room. The* LAWYER *notices them.*

—Oh I just throw my clothes anywhere, that's me.
Sorry I'm not quite ready for you . . .

LAWYER. It's OK; I don't want to push you. I just came to tell
you it's perfectly all right for you to see Ralph tomorrow.

TONI. Oh I've seen him.

LAWYER. Really? But surely you missed the visiting hours.

TONI. I know I did, but they were very obliging. I, um, gave
them a little breakdown, you know—very maternal and all
that. Men can never resist a woman's tears, can they?

LAWYER. Still I'm surprised.

TONI. Well there's usually a gentleman, isn't there? No matter
where you go in the world. You know, I think they're all
gentlemen really, at heart. You've just got to bring it out.
Yes, there's always one.
I'll just get dressed and we'll go downstairs, OK? Help
yourself to one of those drinks; I don't know what they are
but you might find something you like.

She goes to her bathroom. The LAWYER *looks at the tray of drinks.*

Scene Seven

The hotel bar.
It is a sterile sort of room, with one or two ethnic knick-knacks. There is a

well-stocked bar, where the BARMAN *(him from the previous scene) is working—cutting up lemons, cleaning tables, etc.*
The only customer at the moment is LILLY. *She is seated on a stool at the bar, slumped, smoking. She has a beer. She's fed-up, half-drunk. But she can't help admiring the* BARMAN; *she watches him as he moves about—although she is careful never to let him notice.*

LILLY *(finally)*. Excuse me. Can I have another please?

BARMAN. Same again?

LILLY. You haven't got no English beer, have you?

BARMAN. Er . . . sometimes we got Guinness.

LILLY. Oh yeah? Guinness. Guinness is good for you!

BARMAN. Huh?

LILLY. Guinness is good for you! Didn't you know that?

BARMAN. We're out of it right now. I could look in the other bar . . .

LILLY. No no no, you stay there, don't worry. I'll have what I had last time. I feel like something cold, don't I? Something long and cold, know what I mean?

BARMAN. I don't know.

LILLY. No, I don't actually like Guinness.

BARMAN. We don't have Guinness.

LILLY. No, I know—it's all right, come on.

BARMAN. You want same again?

LILLY. Yeah.
    Is it always as hot as this?

BARMAN. Hot?

LILLY. Yeah, I'm saying—is it always as hot as this?

BARMAN. This is the rainy season right now.

LILLY. Yeah? It's always the rainy season at home.

BARMAN. Excuse me, I can't understand what you say. Are you English?

LILLY. 'Course I'm English.

BARMAN. You staying upstairs, yeah?

LILLY. That's right—in Room 433, got it? 433.

BARMAN. How you like?

LILLY. I like it. You mean the room? The room's all right—I wondered what you was talking about there. It's all right. But we ain't here to have a good time, are we? Do you understand?

BARMAN. Er, sure—I don't know.

LILLY. No, we're here to have a bad time, see. It's not a holiday—comprendo? I mean it's only right, really, ennit?

She drinks. He watches her thoughtfully for a while.

BARMAN. Hey.

LILLY. What?

BARMAN. Hey, you wanna score?

LILLY. Wanna score; what d'you mean—score what?

BARMAN. I don't know.

LILLY. Sorry, I'm not with you . . . You mean my room number?

BARMAN. 433, yeah, I got it.

LILLY. Well . . .

BARMAN. I can get you H. You know. (*Mimes needle in arm.*) I can get you cocaine; I can get grass, whatever you want.

LILLY *looks at him then laughs ironically.*

BARMAN. It's not me, you know, but I can get it. You just tell me. What's so goddamned funny? Did I say something funny?

LILLY. Yeah you did, as a matter of fact.

BARMAN. OK, crazy.

LILLY. Yeah it's crazy, ennit pal? The whole fucking thing's crazy, ennit?

BARMAN. OK, you want something I'm around. Tell your husband.

LILLY. My husband, eh? (*Laughs.*)

BARMAN. I don't understand you.

LILLY. Well I understand you, so that's all right, ennit?

> BARMAN *tires of her and goes away—but he remains on stage.*

—(*To herself*). Tell your husband! It's a fucking laugh, ennit?

She lights another cigarette. Coughs.
The LAWYER *and* TONI *come in.* TONI *is well-dressed now—lots of chains and jewellery, etc. She makes quite an impression—or she would if the bar were to be crowded.*
At the start LILLY *doesn't see them and the* BARMAN *is away in another area of the stage.*
The two women make straight for a table.

TONI (*coming in*). No, have you ever tried to fly from Marbella to Penang in a hurry?

LAWYER. I can't say I have . . .

TONI. Take my advice, love—don't . . . We'll sit here, shall we? I feel as though I've been through a spin-dryer. I had to leave in such a hurry—I could only leave a note for Steven—that's my husband, you know. Ralph's stepfather. He's away on business as usual.

LAWYER. What's his line?

TONI. Oh well he, um, diversifies. He moves around a lot. What you having, love?

LAWYER. I'm not really a drinking lady . . .

TONI. Oh, go on, keep me company.

LAWYER. . . . But I think perhaps after a hard day.

TONI. That's the way.

LAWYER. I'll get them. (*To distant* BARMAN.) Excuse me? Excuse me.
Tsk, I know he can hear me . . .

TONI (*without raising her voice*). Waiter.

The BARMAN *comes over.*

—Good evening. I'll have a Jack Collins—can you make one?

BARMAN. Er . . .

TONI. Well go and look it up in your book, love. A Jack Collins for me and—?

LAWYER. I'll have a Tiger.

TONI. A what?

BARMAN. You got it.

TONI. All right—a Tiger for my friend's tank. And bring some nuts or something, will you please?

BARMAN. Nuts?

TONI. Yes, nuts.

He goes.

TONI. I think he's more at his ease with room service.

LAWYER. He does have an insolent way about him. It's because we are women.

TONI. Well I think the young should be insolent; they must find the rest of us so boring.
Do you smoke, Katie?

LAWYER. No thank you.

TONI. Good girl.

She lights up. Coughs.

—No, I've always kept on the move, you know. Still and running water, and all that. I feel it's best that way, what with my temperament. That poor boy's just the same, a rolling stone. But the problem with Ralph, I think, is that he's got the restless nature but he's never had the energy to go with it. And you need one for the other, don't you?

LAWYER. It's a perfect tragedy, isn't it?

TONI. What, about Ralph? Mm.

She brings out a tiny handkerchief and dabs her eyes with it. It is a dubious, theatrical gesture. The LAWYER watches her.

—Still, there you are; we all do these things. There's only one way to stay out of trouble in life and that's stop at home in front of the telly, isn't it? And I'm afraid Ralph broke the golden rule, didn't he?

LAWYER. What's that?

TONI. Don't get caught.

LAWYER. Ah yes.

TONI. I mean to say, really. Having smack in your pants at Penang airport—you've only got to read the papers. It's almost as though he was wanting to get caught, d'you know what I mean?

LAWYER. It was a most unnecessary risk.

TONI. Well there you are. But I told him, I said to him—you've always been unworldly, just like your father.

LAWYER. When did you say this to him?

TONI. This afternoon.
His name was Jack Collins, you know—his father. That's why I drink them. It's all that's left of poor old Jack, an old bat sat drinking cocktails in Marbella.

BARMAN *brings the drinks.*

—Ah, speak of the devil. The devil drink. That looks as though it might have some resemblance to what I asked for. Well done, young man.

BARMAN. I worked in the States for a year.

TONI. Oh a Tiger's a beer, is it? That's a good idea . . .

BARMAN. Nuts.

TONI. Oh yes, thank you.

The BARMAN's *insolent presence has irritated the* LAWYER. *She mutters something stern to him in Malay.*
He goes, swinging away.

TONI. Eh, I think you said the wrong thing to him there, Katie. You know, I bet you're a handful when you're crossed; I bet you are.

LAWYER. I don't like him.

TONI. You don't have to, do you? He's only a skivvy.

LAWYER (*smiles*). I had forgotten that word.

TONI. Here's to better times!

LAWYER. Better times!

Pause while they drink.

TONI. I'm a monkey; that's why I always ask for nuts.

LAWYER. Sorry?

TONI. I was born in the year of the monkey. You know, the Chinese calendar. What are you?

LAWYER. I've really no idea.

TONI. Horse, I'd say.

LAWYER. You can tell these things?

TONI. Oh yes—you're definitely a horse.

LAWYER. Perhaps I should ask him to bring me some oats.

TONI. Oats! Eh, that's very good, love. Oh thank God I've got a lawyer who's a human being.

LAWYER. Actually I am not like this at all; I'm very stuffy.

TONI (*going straight on*). Now I'll tell you what I was thinking, shall I?

LAWYER. Sorry?

TONI. I want to put my proposition to you.

LAWYER. Oh yes. Please.

TONI (*her manner has changed*). Now I don't want you to get the wrong idea about me, all right? I don't want you to think I'm trying to shock you or anything. This is strictly business. But I do want to know what you think.

LAWYER. OK.

TONI. Now as I understand it, the appeal has to go through two stages. First to the Parliament, then to the Governor. And you say the first usually fails, all right . . .

LAWYER. I'm afraid so . . .

TONI. Now the Governor. It'll then be up to him, right?

LAWYER. His decision is very crucial.

TONI. Quite. (*Eats a nut.*) And he'll be a man, of course?

LAWYER. Oh yes.

TONI. Now I believe, Katie, that in life each of us should play to our strengths and disguise our weaknesses, you know. I mean if you're rich, for example, you should use your money. You'd be soft not to. If you're very strong—and so on. (*Eats another nut.*) I wonder if I could get to see him?

LAWYER. The Governor? It's possible he would give you an appointment.

TONI. Hm. He hangs my son and it's possible he'd give me an appointment. Never mind—what was I saying? Yes, I'm going to put it to you straight, Katie because you've got a lot of human qualities and, well, because there's no one else, quite frankly.

LAWYER. OK.

TONI. What if I managed to get to see this Governor at his office—maybe even his home—and I offered myself to him? I mean, I think I'm justified in thinking he'd find me reasonably attractive, don't you?

LAWYER. I'm not sure you're serious.

TONI. You don't think it's a good idea?

LAWYER. You want to—but it doesn't work like that at all.

TONI. What doesn't, love?

LAWYER. Why, the legal system.

TONI. I'm not talking about the legal system, am I? I'm talking about an older system than that. The world is run by men, Katie, with all due respect to your good self. And let's face it, men want one thing and one thing only.

LAWYER. Are you really serious?

TONI. Absolutely.

LAWYER. You want to flirt around with the *Governor?*

TONI. Well, that's putting it very demurely; I'm a little surprised at you, Katie.

LAWYER. Oh *you're* surprised at *me?*

TONI. I'll give him what he wants and he gives me what I want.

LAWYER: The Governor is a married man with grown-up children and everything.

TONI *laughs*.

LAWYER. He's a Muslim.

TONI (*laughs louder*). Don't Muslims do it then?

LAWYER. I've never heard anything so outrageous in all my life.

TONI. No well you're young yet. I thought I'd just float the idea, you know.

LAWYER. I don't believe I'm hearing this actually.

TONI. Don't get me wrong, love; I'm not saying it's something I'd enjoy doing. I expect it would be pretty nasty. I can just imagine what he's like. But we are talking about a human life, aren't we? If it were anything else it would be a different matter. My own son.

LAWYER. But what a . . . Look, I've lived in England, you know. I studied at Cambridge and everything, so I know about the English sense of humour—but assuming you're serious— assuming that, I say . . . What a very low opinion you must have of us! I mean to say, would you consider such a step if it was in England?

TONI. Ah well it doesn't quite hold up, that argument, I'm afraid love because in England we've done away with the death penalty, haven't we? For better or worse. But what I think is—if you are dealing with barbarians you've got to use barbarian tactics.

LAWYER. Barbarians.

TONI *says nothing. She eats a nut.*

—You know this is a terrible insult.

TONI. It's just between you and me; I did warn you. Why are you taking it personally?

LAWYER. I am a member of the society you are insulting.

TONI. Are you?

LAWYER. Yes.

TONI. People can say anything about England to me, I don't bat an eye. Silly, isn't it?

All right, come on—forget I said anything.

She drinks.

LAWYER. But I would say you also have a very low opinion of women.

TONI. You're probably dead right there, love.

LAWYER. To debase yourself like that; to even think of it. Excuse me, but to use sex in that way . . .

TONI. Well, there's quite a bit of it about, you know. Sex. They use it here, don't they? It's only using what I've got to get what I want. To save a life.

LAWYER. Well it wouldn't work.

TONI. All right.

LAWYER. We do have a legal system, you know.

TONI. Yes well you've got the British to thank for that, haven't you?

LAWYER (*bowing*). Thank you very much.

TONI. No, you stick to the text-book, love, and you're doomed; the law is just one big text-book, isn't it? It's like that guerrilla warfare, what I'm talking about. If you don't do something—underhand—you're buggered, aren't you? I'll have another please. (*Signals to* BARMAN.)—You're not keeping up with your Tiger, love.

LAWYER. I feel like crying.

TONI. Ah. (*Eats nut.*) That's another woman's guile, isn't it?

LAWYER. You have a very cynical view of women.

TONI. Ooh, you should hear me once I get started on men. He's a Muslim, you say?

LAWYER. Hm?

TONI. This Governor chappie. You say he's a Muslim. Does he have ten wives?

LAWYER. You are thinking of another country entirely.

TONI. Am I? Ooh my geography's terrible.

LAWYER. You know I should walk out of that door.

TONI *says nothing.*

—But I won't because I think you need me. I think you need me very much.

TONI (*blandly*). Yes.

LAWYER. You know I'm very sorry you've raised this—topic because I wanted you to listen to what I had to say about Ralph and Bryan.

TONI. Oh yes?

From now on LILLY *listens to what is said.*

LAWYER. Well, first—in Ralph's case, as distinct from Bryan's case, I should say that there is a somewhat better chance of a successful appeal.

TONI. Really? How's that?

LAWYER. Well you know Ralph is a registered addict. The amount he had on him was very small and I believe in Court we were able to prove that it was for his personal use. They didn't believe it but they couldn't altogether discount it. Of course, he was with Bryan—who had a substantial amount, and Ralph was a member of a syndicate—that's undeniable, but what I'm saying is there's some hope there.

TONI (*a beat*). A registered addict.

LAWYER. Hm?

TONI. Ralph's a registered addict, you say?

LAWYER. Yes.

TONI. Of heroin? I didn't know that. The things you find out, eh?

LAWYER. Well it may sound strange, but it is all to the good for us at this juncture.

TONI. Oh the appeal, yes.

LAWYER. Also, and perhaps more hopefully—I guess you'll know that lawyers and judges can do a lot of behind-the-scenes work? Well, this is not definite, you know, but it's certain that Ralph knows more about this syndicate than he is telling. He knows who is at the head of it and everything. In court he categorically refused to name names, but—well, I believe the door is still open for him.

TONI. You mean all he has to do is name the Mr Big sort of thing?

LAWYER. Yes, here in Malaysia. That's what they want.

TONI. And he's refused to?

LAWYER. Yes, so far.

TONI. And if he names him they'll let him off?

LAWYER. Nothing is certain. It won't do us any harm.

TONI (*to* BARMAN). Have you got that Jack Collins yet please? I'll speak to him.

LAWYER. Good.

TONI. If that's the way it works, the 'system'.

LAWYER. It's the same in every country; deals are made.

TONI. Yes.

LAWYER. In England too.

TONI. Yes I'm sure. (*She smiles at her.*)

LAWYER. Well I suppose I'd better be pushing off—my husband will be home.

TONI. Oh I hope it's not too late for you to get to the shops.

LAWYER. Thank you for the drink.

TONI. Oh the Tiger, yes. It's all right; I'm glad I was able to tempt you.

The LAWYER *looks at her curiously; she can't make* TONI *out.* TONI *smiles back.*

—Until tomorrow, then.

LAWYER. Yes. Don't worry, hm?

TONI. Thank you so much.

Their goodbye is interrupted by the BARMAN, *who comes over and serves* TONI *her drink. While* TONI *thanks him the* LAWYER *leaves.*
LILLY *is now watching* TONI. *She's a bit wobbly on her stool.*

TONI. Ah, yes, just put it down there will you?

The BARMAN *allows his hand to pass across her shoulder as he walks away.* TONI *shows no sign of noticing.*
LILLY *now comes over to* TONI's *table. She is none too sure of her footing and slurs a bit.*

LILLY. Hello.

TONI. Oh hello . . .

LILLY. All right?

TONI. Yes, I'm all right.

LILLY. D'you mind if I?

> TONI *gestures for her to sit down.*
> *She does so and immediately seems to enter a reverie.*

—Sorry, I'm Bryan's sister.

TONI. Oh I see, I wondered . . . How do you do? I'm Ralph's mother. Well I expect you know that.

LILLY. Yeah. Sorry, I've had a few.

TONI. It's all right, love.

LILLY. Look like piddle but they don't half go to your head. Still—eh?

TONI. Yes. So are you here with your parents?

LILLY. Yeah. They're upstairs looking after my kid.

> LILLY *doesn't expand on this but she stretches out her legs and arms and heaves a sigh of relief.* TONI *watches her.*

LILLY *(finally)*. I haven't got a husband.

TONI. It's all right, love; it's got nothing to do with me.

LILLY. No, I'm just saying. I ain't got anybody. *(She laughs oddly.)* How d'you fancy that?

> *She nods at the* BARMAN.
> TONI *says nothing.*

—I had a boyfriend, obviously. That's obvious, ennit? You know what he done, him?

TONI. Who, your boyfriend?

LILLY. No, *him*. *(The* BARMAN.*)*

TONI. No.

LILLY. I was sat over there, having a drink, right? He comes up, he goes 'Hey, you want heroin?'

TONI *says nothing but she takes this in.*

—Yeah, I was sitting there—straight, he only offers me heroin, cocaine, hash, I dunno what.

TONI. Really?

LILLY. You know what I thought? I thought—what's Bryan dying for? I mean when it's freely available, you know what I mean?

TONI. It's very ironic.

LILLY. Ennit?

TONI. Mm.

LILLY. I mean they're just walking about the streets here. You been outside yet?

TONI. No, love; I get all my pleasures indoors.

LILLY. You walk hundred yards, guaranteed you get offered heroin, opium, cocaine. It's pathetic—they're doing this to Bryan and people like that just for the publicity. Like they're making out they ain't got no drug problem.

TONI. That boy should certainly watch his step.

LILLY. Who, Bryan? It's a bit late for that, isn't it?

TONI. No, him.

LILLY. Oh him, I couldn't care less about him. I was just making a point, that's all. Here, shall I report him to the Manager?

TONI. No.

LILLY. I've a good mind to. Maybe I could get him hung as well.

TONI. Sleep on it, eh?

LILLY. Yeah and all that bollocks she give you: (*Attempts the* LAWYER*'s accent.*) 'I think Ralph has a better chance of getting off than Bryan . . .' It's exactly what she said to us. Only with Bryan having a better chance than Ralph! Straight, exactly the same.

Pause. TONI *eats a nut.*

I hope you don't mind—I weren't listening-in. I wasn't
listening; it's just when I heard her mention Bryan's name.
Who'd wanna come here, eh? For pleasure, sort of thing?
What is it, part of China really? I meant to get pissed tonight;
I hope you don't mind. I open up when I've had a few—as
the actress said to the bishop!
Cor, I'll give him that, though—he's the first tasty thing I
seen since I got here, including the food. Pity he's a pusher. I
used to have a boyfriend who was a pusher, bastard. I think
that's the worst thing in the world to be, don't you?
He's got a nice arse, though, give him that.
Have you seen your boy yet?

TONI *nods.*

—I'm surprised; they're quite easy-going really, at the prison,
I thought. I went to visit someone in Pentonville once. Well,
and Brixton. They're much worse than here. Makes you
think—it would be quite easy to slip him something, I
reckon. I could put it in the baby's what's'isnames. He could
sort of hold the baby and gurgle over it an' that and—what
d'you think? Think it's worth a try?

TONI. Why not?

LILLY. It's only fair, ennit? If they're going to have these
ridiculous laws. Gives him a chance, dunnit? 'Cos it ain't
gonna work, is it, this appeal thing? We all know that, don't
we? 'Cept my dad—he seems to think we'll all be going
home together and it'll be straight down the pub. But they
did hang them Australian boys, didn't they? It's all this
national pride shit these foreigners have got, fucking idiots.

TONI. The question is—would he have the guts to use it?

LILLY. What, the knife? Yeah. He did cut Gary that time. That's
my boyfriend—well, ex-boyfriend. He beat me within an inch
of my life, so Bryan went round there and give him a stripe.

TONI. A what?

LILLY. A stripe. (*She gestures: cut down the face.*) I dunno what he
can do. Sort of get a gun or something . . . It's only fair he
should get a chance, that's what I think.

TONI. No, what I meant was . . .

LILLY. Yeah, sorry . . .

TONI. Don't you think he might use it on himself?

LILLY. Himself? I hadn't thought of that.

TONI. Or, worse still—on the other boy?

LILLY. Well, we got to do something, haven't we? We can't just stand by and let a bunch of wogs hang our boys. (*To the* BARMAN.) Yeah, that means you an' all! (*To* TONI.) We got to do something, haven't we?

TONI. I tell you what—sleep on it. And do something for me, will you?

LILLY. What's that?

TONI. Call me Toni. Everyone in Marbella calls me Toni. All right?

LILLY. Yeah.

TONI. That's a good girl. Night night.

   TONI *gets up and goes.*

LILLY (*to herself*). Toni. That's a nice name. Used to know someone called that. (*To* BARMAN.) All right?

   She and the BARMAN *stand looking at each other as the lights go down.*

End of Act One

ACT TWO

Scene One

The visiting room at the prison.
BRYAN *is holding the baby, on his side of the desk. Opposite,* GEORGE,
WENDY *and* LILLY.
The GAOLER *(and if possible other guards) watching closely.*
There is no visible sign of a knife being passed over, via the baby. LILLY
watches but her features are glazed, as ever.

BRYAN. Funny looking thing, isn't he? How's it feel to be on the
wrong side of the law, mate? Eh? How's it feel to be a
hardened criminal? Yeah? Look, he's smiling, isn't he? Or
else he's crapped himself.

GEORGE. He does smile a lot, don't he Wend? For his age, like.

BRYAN. Here, he hasn't *been* has he? Let's have a look . . .

GEORGE. Yeah, they always go on me, Bry—funny that. Only got
to pick 'em up and . . . whoops. It must be some sort of
property I got in my make-up, sort of thing, ennit Wend?

WENDY. It's the only property you have got.

GEORGE. Yeah that's true! *(He laughs and coughs.)* Cor, yeah, I see
what you mean about the upset tummy, Bry. I've had it ever
since we arrived, haven't I Wend?

WENDY. Yeah.

GEORGE. She'll tell you. It's a good thing we got an adjoining
toilet 'cos I don't think I'd've made it a couple of times,
would I Wend?

WENDY. No.

BRYAN. You got me all in tears, entcha?

GEORGE. Got them Lomotil that the doctor give us but I don't
think they do any good really. There's nothing as good as
antibodies.

BRYAN. Whole fucking place is anti-body, ennit?

LILLY. You ain't got room in you for no more pills.

GEORGE. Yeah, that's true! (*Laughs and coughs.*) Bleedin' cough . . .

BRYAN. Here you are, take him back . . .

Passes the baby back to LILLY.

LILLY. All right?

BRYAN. Very nice.

Pause. No one knows what to say.

So what about this MP of yours, then? What's he gonna do?

GEORGE (*beginning*). Well . . .

WENDY. It's too late; it's just the Prime Minister now.

BRYAN. Yeah. Funny, ennit? I mean they ought to make drugs legal and put an end to all this once and for all. Then them that wants 'em can have 'em and you don't get pushers and people corrupting minors and mugging little old ladies an' that to support their habit. Stands to reason. When they gonna bring this in? They're thinking about it in America, it's gotta come. Fifty years from now no one's gonna believe they done this; they're gonna say fuck me that's completely outrageous like not letting women have the vote an' that. I mean I'm only 20, aren't I? Are you sure everyone understands that? I been trying to get that across to 'em but I'm not sure it's what's'isname—registered. I'm not sure they registered the fact. Tell them I'm only 20.

GEORGE. Yeah all right Bry; I'll tell them at the office . . .

BRYAN. So what about the Prime Minister, then? She's supposed to be popular with the rest of the world, isn't she? Always poncing off abroad and meeting blacks an' that . . . Her word's got to mean something, I would've thought.

GEORGE. Oh definitely. Say what you like about her, the rest of the world leaders look up to her, don't they Wend? Apparently she's the only foreign head of state that Americans have heard of, even. I was reading about it in . . .

BRYAN. Well why don't she come out here then? They're not gonna turn her down to her face, are they? I mean I'd fucking do it. If it was an Englishman being held by foreigners, 'course I would. Wouldn't matter what he'd done. 'Cos I got pride in my country. It ain't no trouble for her, is it? I mean the Government pays for her, dunnit?

GEORGE. Yeah, plus she'd get some free publicity out of it. I'm sure all this has been taken into due consideration, Bry—I mean we got no idea what's going on behind the scenes, have we Wend?

BRYAN. Yeah well if only they'd bloody tell us something. Goin' mad in here. Give us a smoke, for Christ's sake.

GEORGE *gives him a cigarette. His hands are shaking, much worse than* BRYAN's. *In fact* BRYAN *has to take hold of* GEORGE's *in order to get the light. It's a small moment of tenderness which passes quickly.*

BRYAN. Didn't I need that.

GEORGE. You are getting enough fags and that, I hope Bry? because I did . . .

BRYAN. Yeah, yeah, I just left 'em behind, didn't I? Funny, no one pinches our fags now.

GEORGE. Yeah? Why's that? Oh—yeah.

Pause.

BRYAN. Dunno what to talk about, do I?

WENDY. I'm sorry, I . . .

BRYAN. No, no, it's all right.

WENDY. What about the other boy? How's he?

BRYAN. He's all right. Don't show his feelings much.

WENDY. His mother's at the same hotel . . .

BRYAN. Yeah well he's a cunt, isn't he?

WENDY. . . . she's on the same floor.

GEORGE (*picking up from* BRYAN). Yeah well she's an unusual woman.

LILLY. What do you mean she's an unusual woman?

GEORGE. What I say, she's . . .

LILLY. Yeah well it don't mean nothing, do it? Unusual woman— what's it mean, she's got two heads or something?

GEORGE. What I mean . . .

LILLY. You don't know what you fucking mean.

GEORGE. If you'll just let me finish . . .

LILLY. Oh you haven't finished yet? I thought you said she was an unusual woman—I thought that was it.

GEORGE. I was going on to say . . .

LILLY. You're *always* bleedin' going on . . .

GEORGE. May I?

LILLY. 'Course.

GEORGE. Is it all right with you?

LILLY. Feel free.

GEORGE. Thank you.

LILLY. It's all right.

GEORGE. She must have had him very young.

LILLY. Not necessarily.

GEORGE. She can't be more than 45, Lil.

LILLY. She's 40, she told me.

GEORGE. Yeah well there you are, that's quite young, ennit? Oh I see what you mean now . . . Not as young as you, eh?

LILLY (*making a simpering face*). 'Not as young as you eh?'

BRYAN. Shut up, will you?

LILLY. Sorry Bry, but he's really been winding me up, you know what I mean?

BRYAN. I'm the one who's fucking wound up aren't I?

GEORGE. Yeah, sorry, Bry.

BRYAN. I mean you can do all this when you get home, can't you? You can fucking tear each other to bits then.

LILLY. Not me mate; I won't be there.

GEORGE. Oh really? You've found yourself a flat, have you?

LILLY. Maybe.

GEORGE. Oh that's very interesting Lilly; you must tell me all about that.

By now they realise that WENDY *has been driven very low by all this. She isn't actually crying but she's obviously very demoralised.*

BRYAN. One thing I won't miss. Oh yeah, there is something. Listen. About the papers . . .

GEORGE. Oh yeah, we wanted to . . .

LILLY. Shut up . . .

BRYAN. Will you *listen*! About the papers: I don't mind, all right? It just come as a shock when you told me, that's all, but I been thinking about it and I want to say I don't mind. I don't blame you; I'd do the same, wouldn't I? Just make sure you sting 'em for every bastard penny that's all. Bleedin' vultures.

WENDY. I do feel awful about that.

GEORGE. They caught us on the hop, I suppose it was really. What do they call it? Doorstepping, ennit?

LILLY. Shut up . . .

BRYAN. You should go back to England. If it happens it happens, fuck it.

GEORGE. 'Course, the other thing is the Queen.

LILLY. What's she gonna do? Hit 'em with her handbag?

GEORGE. No, they listen to her, don't they? Because this used to be a colony, didn't it? You know there are some places here, they still believe Queen Victoria's alive.

LILLY. Oh that's useful.

GEORGE. No, what I'm saying is—there's a lingering affection.

LILLY. Lingering affliction.

GEORGE. I'm just trying to be positive, thank you Lilly.

LILLY. Oh is that what it is? Thanks for telling me.

GEORGE. We've just got no idea what's going on.

LILLY. That's the truest word you said yet, mate.

BRYAN (*To* WENDY). Oi, listen, you know my room? I dunno if it's still my room—what *was* my room. I got these—I dunno—stories and songs an' that in there, right? Shit like that, done 'em when I was a kid, didn't I? Well, they're in the drawers, right?
(*To the others.*) You don't have to listen to this. (*To* WENDY.) They're in the drawers, in the bedroom; they're hidden in the drawers in all these exercise books, right? They're easy to find; they're just shoved up the back. It's just old bollocks, stories and songs like what every kid writes. Do me a favour, right? Get 'em out and chuck 'em away. And don't read them! I mean it—I'm deadly serious; don't even look at them. It's the most serious thing I ever asked, right? I really don't want you to even cast your eyes over them. Just chuck 'em straight out. All right?

GEORGE (*a beat*). Yeah all right, Bry.

LILLY. He wasn't talking to you.

WENDY. I know.

BRYAN. Thank you. (*Then.*) What d'you mean you know?

WENDY. I've always known they're there.

BRYAN. What, always?

WENDY. Yeah.

BRYAN. Well why didn't you say?

WENDY. Because they were private to you. Because you hid them.

BRYAN. You knew they was there but you never said nothing?

WENDY. Well I knew they were private to you, didn't I?

BRYAN. Yeah I know, but—why didn't you tell me?

WENDY. Because . . .

BRYAN. You read 'em!

WENDY. I looked through them.

BRYAN. You looked through 'em—my private things and you never mentioned it! You must've put 'em back just how you found 'em. I mean if you'd seen 'em why didn't you

encourage me? Eh? I mean all I needed was a bit of
encouragement, wasn't it?

LILLY. Encouragement? You must be joking mate.

BRYAN. Don't you understand anything? I could have been
something. How d'you know that wasn't a gold-mine in
there? I could have been something—a fucking song-writer,
or something. Instead of the cunt I am.

GEORGE. Shh, never mind now.

BRYAN. I dunno—I just don't get the point, do I? I mean I
obviously just don't sort of—get it. Fucking best thing for me,
I reckon. (*To* GAOLER.) You reckon that, don't you Abdul?
Win a ticket in a raffle, cunt don't even know what country
he's going to! I tell you a secret—I don't even know where I
am! They tried to show me on the atlas once; I couldn't be
bothered to look. (*Laughs.*) Fucking Martian's got more idea
than I have. Where am I, d'you know?

GEORGE. Well it's Malaysia, Bry.

BRYAN. Ta, Dad.

He stands up.

—I dunno if this is gonna be the last time or what . . .

The GAOLER *whispers to him.*

—He says I got to say goodbye, just to be on the safe side.
Nice way of saying things, haven't they? Not definite, but . . .

They embrace one by one.

BRYAN (*to* LILLY). Take care of yourself, girl.

LILLY. Might be seeing you, eh?

BRYAN. I don't think you know what it's like, actually.
(*To* WENDY.) See you Mum; just try and forget it, eh?
(*To* GEORGE.) Dad. What a bastard, isn't it?

He goes.

GEORGE. Come on. We'd better go and see if there's any
developments.

WENDY. Hang on, wait a minute—I never said . . . He's just
gone, hasn't he? I wanted to say something to him.

GEORGE. Come on.

LILLY lingers.

GEORGE. Come on then, Lil.

LILLY. Fucking Pakis.

She goes.

The stage is empty, then TONI *comes in.*
She goes and sits where WENDY *had been sitting. She waits.*
RALPH is brought in by the GAOLER, *led in wrist-chains.*
He sits where BRYAN *had been sitting.*
He kisses her on the cheeks.

RALPH. Apparently this could be the last time, although stays of execution are sometimes, you know . . .

TONI. It's all happened so fast.

RALPH (*imitating hysterical female*). 'It all happened so fast officer!' I hope your cats are all right.

TONI. My cats are all right.

RALPH. Pity I never got out to the old hacienda.

TONI. It's a pity we—lost contact. I'm sorry, I've not been leading a very reputable life.

RALPH. It's all right; this is not your confessional.

TONI. No, I just.

RALPH. It's not your fault; you're just too young to be a parent, I guess.

TONI (*smiling*). Yes.

RALPH. So what you reading at the moment? Always got a book on the go, my old ma.

TONI. I only ever read one book, love. *I Ching.*

RALPH. Really? What does it say?

TONI. I haven't asked it.

RALPH. No, good idea.

TONI. Let's be businesslike . . .

RALPH. Oh yes, let's. Sorry, was I getting a bit emotional there? I expect the pressure's getting to me, by God!

TONI. I want you to tell them the names you know.

RALPH. Ah. Yes, I believe there was something about this in Court.

TONI. Tell them the names. That's all they want. I know for a fact.

RALPH. You do?

TONI. They don't want to do this to you.

RALPH. Yes I've noticed their marked reluctance. Well they don't have to on my account, you know.

TONI. So just tell them the names. It's only one or two they want—the man who supplies in Malaya; they don't care about Australia or America.

RALPH. I'm just the small fry, am I?

TONI. So you see there's no point in protecting them, is there? They're not doing anything for you.

RALPH. I don't know; they might be tunnelling under here right now.

TONI. You only have to . . .

RALPH. You know you're very naïve. They can't go back now. The whole thing's been set in motion. Officials have been assigned; the front page is being held. Sell your story like the other guy's parents . . .

TONI. You know I would do anything for you. Anything.

RALPH. OK.

TONI. I've even suggested one or two things but on balance they appeared to be counterproductive . . .

RALPH. What if I gave them the names and they *still* hang me?

GAOLER. Ralph, listen to your mother.

TONI. That's a risk.

RALPH. It is, isn't it? Ah, they want to hang me. They've got the taste. Besides, what about the other kid? I go free and he swings? Even I wouldn't pull a stroke like that. How d'you know I was in here? Get the *Daily Mail* out in Spain, do you?

TONI. Just tell them the names. Tell me if you like.

RALPH. Tell *you*? Are you kidding? God knows what you'd do with my contacts.

TONI. Tell me the names. Just one name.

RALPH. Oh we're down to one name now. You're compromising already.

TONI. Tell me the names.

RALPH. That's more like it. Mickey Mouse.

TONI. Tell me the names.

RALPH. What's in a name? You get the name but you don't get the person, do you? Not the essential . . .

TONI. You've only got to tell me a name; they'll never know— just tell me the names.

RALPH. Blah-blah.

TONI. Come on, tell me the names. (*Pause.*) Tell me the names. (*Pause.*) Tell me. Tell me the . . .

RALPH. Oh stop saying that; it's getting monotonous. And it isn't the point, you know. It really isn't.

TONI. Tell me the names.

RALPH. Jesus.

TONI (*she's very calm*). Tell me a name. Whisper it in my ear.

RALPH. We're not allowed to whisper.

TONI. Tell me a name and leave the rest to me . . .

RALPH. I don't know any names! OK? They're not that dumb— it's all done through a whole system of middlemen; you don't even get to meet them. I've only met other schmucks like me, and they've passed on. I only let them go on thinking I know names because—who knows? Because I want them to think it, OK? Maybe I wanted them to think I'm somebody. Somebody more than I am. So it isn't the point, see? Am I making myself clear now? I know nothing—there's no way out.

TONI. Make up a name. Anyone you half know, anyone you know. It'll buy you time.

RALPH. Anyone I know or half-know? OK, I'll give you a name. You ready? Ralph. How about that.

He stands up and prepares to go out.
TONI *stands up quickly.*

GAOLER. Ralph! Kiss your mother.

RALPH (*returning*). He's a big family man, you know. These Sikhs are like that; they don't understand us, our—understatement and all that shit. (*He laughs.*) Something rather universal, kind of eternal in this scene, don't you think? Mothers and their sons—you can't beat it.

He goes to give her a peck on the cheek but somehow the embrace very quickly becomes impassioned: she covers him with kisses and they hold each other tightly.

TONI (*calling out his name, etc*). !! (*adding in a final whisper*) I love you, I think the other boy's got a knife!

RALPH is taken away. They separate reluctantly.

Scene Two

The prison cell.
It is very hot. BRYAN *and* RALPH *are slumped on their separate bunks, with their shirts open. No chains.*
With them is the GAOLER. *He is a bit dozy.*

BRYAN. Oi shit-for-brains, talking fast, all right?

RALPH. What?

BRYAN. Talking *fast* all right?

RALPH. OK.

They speak very fast and colloquially.

BRYAN. I got a blade.

RALPH. Yeah I know.

BRYAN. How d'you *know*?

RALPH. What is it?

BRYAN. Like a kitchen knife, about six inches, sharp as a bastard.

RALPH (*a little too clearly*). What do you want to do with it?

BRYAN. Careful!

RALPH. All right . . .

BRYAN. Dozy bastard . . . Dunno, do I. Thought you might have some ideas, full of ideas, you are, as a rule.

RALPH. We wouldn't get past the door.

BRYAN. I know we wouldn't.

RALPH. Even if we got the gun off him.

BRYAN. I know.

RALPH. You weren't thinking of that, were you?

BRYAN. I don't know. I ain't completely stupid.

RALPH. So what do you want to do with it?

BRYAN. I'm thinking, aren't I? Fucking do him with it, couldn't I?

The GAOLER *looks at* BRYAN; BRYAN *smiles at him.*

—All right?

GAOLER. What language are you talking?

BRYAN. It's English, isn't it? You don't know everything, do you?

GAOLER. You're crazy boy.

BRYAN (*To* RALPH *but looking at* GAOLER) Shall I give him a stripe down his face?

RALPH. Don't be dumb.

BRYAN. Got a better idea, have you? Could do, couldn't I? (*To* GAOLER) No, you don't know what we're talking about, do you? Thought you knew English, didn't you? But you don't, do you?

RALPH. Shut up.

BRYAN. I could fucking scalp him like a chicken. I mean—might as well hang me for something I done, didn't they?

RALPH. You 'done' something.

BRYAN. Met you, that's what I done.

RALPH. Start messing around with these guys, you'll really get it. They'll *hurt* you, d'you understand?

GAOLER. No, not so much 'hurting'—don't worry.

BRYAN. Bloody waste, though, isn't it? I mean maybe we could get as far as the front gates, use the bastard as an 'ostage sort of thing . . . You'd like to smell the fresh air at least, wouldn't you?

RALPH. Yeah.

BRYAN. I mean I gotta do something with it, haven't I?

RALPH. Why?

BRYAN. What d'you mean, why? You're always asking why all the time. What's the matter with you? When you're dead you won't know the fucking difference.

They both laugh.

RALPH. You could just as easily have not come by it, you know.

BRYAN. Yeah well I *did* come by it so shut up. You never, did you? 'Spect you're gonna go along meek as a lamb, aren't you? Yes sir, no sir, shall I put my head in now sir?

RALPH. If you're so desperate to do something with it . . .

BRYAN. I'm sorry I told you about it now . . .

RALPH. . . . You could always do me with it. Really, I give you full permission, anytime you like.

BRYAN. Typical. You scumbag; you're always thinking about yourself, entcha?

GAOLER. What you are giving 'permission' for? What are you talking about?

BRYAN. Can't you be fucking careful.

GAOLER (*to* BRYAN). Hm? What was that? I will bring the chains.

BRYAN. Nothing Mr Guard, sir. We was just saying careful or we'll wake up that nice guard of ours.

GAOLER. I am not sleeping.

BRYAN. (*to* RALPH *again*). No, the only pleasure I got left is seeing you go to that scaffold.

RALPH. Yeah I'd hate to deny you that . . .

BRYAN. That's gonna be so nice to see, I'll tell you . . .

RALPH. . . . I hate to disappoint you but they put hoods over our heads.

BRYAN. Yeah? They tell you that? Fucking hell—that's worse than animals ennit? Even an animal's got more dignity than that. How d'you know that anyway? You always gotta make out you know everything. I suppose you done it before.

RALPH. I've seen it in the movies.

BRYAN. Hilarious. *I* seen it in the movies. It might be different, it's what I'm saying.

RALPH. It's really burning a hole in your pocket. Give it to him.

GAOLER. Give what to me?

BRYAN. Now look what you done.

GAOLER. What have you got?

BRYAN. Satisfied? (*To* GAOLER.) I'll give it to you in your Paki guts, pal.

Pause.

—All right, watch this.

Pause: no one moves.
Then, suddenly, BRYAN *pulls the knife and holds it in striking distance of the* GAOLER.

RALPH. You idiot.

BRYAN. You touch that gun, Abdul, I'm gonna rip your fucking guts open, all right?

GAOLER. OK.

BRYAN. All right?

GAOLER. OK, I understand.

BRYAN. I'm glad you understand. You hear that—somebody understands me all of a sudden. I wonder why that is.

RALPH. So what's next?

BRYAN. Don't touch that gun, all right?

GAOLER. I am not touching it.

RALPH. He's not touching it.

BRYAN. Whose side are you on?

RALPH. I just don't want you to . . .

GAOLER. You know, you will go nowhere with this. It is impossible. They won't let you.

RALPH. He knows that.

BRYAN. Do I? All right maybe I do. All right, tell you what. Say this after me: I am a Paki. Go on—'I am a Paki.'

The GAOLER *speaks calmly, as though humouring a child.*

GAOLER. I am a Paki.

BRYAN. I am the lowest form of life.

GAOLER. I am the lowest form of life.

BRYAN. It's me they should be hanging, not you.

RALPH. Shut up.

GAOLER. It's me they should be hanging, not you.

BRYAN. Bryan.

GAOLER. Bryan.

BRYAN. Right. You can have it now.

He gives the GAOLER *the knife. The* GAOLER *takes it. He bears no resentment.*
BRYAN *sits down again. He buries his head in his hands.*

BRYAN. I'm dead!

Scene Three

The final scene is set in GEORGE *and* WENDY's *hotel room, leading up to the time of the executions.*
However, there are two brief 'cutaway' scenes at the prison.
At the start the room is empty.
After a while, LILLY *comes in from her room. She is wearing nothing much and her hair is tousled. She searches around in a suitcase, finds a carton of*

cigarettes and returns to her room, slamming the door.
Silence until the entrance of WENDY, GEORGE *and* TONI. *They look downcast and exhausted, although* TONI *retains a sense of defiant jauntiness. She has a large duty-free bottle of whisky with her. She pours everyone a stiff one and hands them round.*
They drink without speaking.

TONI. Do you want to put the TV on? I don't know if you'll want it.

WENDY. May as well.

> WENDY *turns on the TV, switching channels. But they all seem to be the same: light music. She leaves it on, with the sound down.*
> *From time to time they all look in its direction to consult it, but there is never a news programme.*
> *They all sit in silence with their drinks.*

TONI. Will you excuse me a minute? I'm just going to my room for something.

> *She goes some way, returns, picks up her bag.*

—Tsk! I'd forget me 'ead!

> *She goes out. Silence again.*

GEORGE. She's a nice woman really, don't you think? I think she's more upset than she looks. I think she probably needs the company, don't you?

> WENDY *doesn't reply; she drinks her glass dry.*

WENDY. Give us another of that.

> GEORGE *gives her more whisky. He looks at the bottle.*

GEORGE. We should've got some of this, but I never saw the place at the airport where you're supposed to get it.

> WENDY *is drinking fast, like a seasoned drinker. They both light cigarettes.*
> GEORGE *stares blankly at the TV screen.*

WENDY. She in there?

GEORGE. I dunno. Want me to look?

> WENDY *doesn't answer, and he doesn't move.*
> GEORGE *holds out his shaking hand.*

—Look at that. It's 'cos I'm expecting that phone to ring any minute isn't it?

WENDY *(with a scoffing laugh)*. Are you?
I weren't hanging around them prison-gates just so the bloody telly could film me.

GEORGE. No.

WENDY. I mean was I?

GEORGE. No. No way.

WENDY. Fuck that. Don't do no good, does it?

GEORGE. No.

WENDY. What have I got to live for?

GEORGE. Yeah.

WENDY. I'm serious. I want to know. What have I got to live for?

GEORGE. Well we'll see when we get back, won't we?

WENDY. Will we?

GEORGE. Yeah well, leave it till then, eh?

WENDY. You bring 'em into this world and what do you get?
Shat on. That's what I am, every way I turn. Shat on. Give us that bottle. Can see you used to work in a pub, the measures you hand out.

GEORGE. Don't overdo it, eh?

WENDY. Bollocks. You look after yourself.

GEORGE. No, I'm just saying, aren't I?

WENDY. Well don't say—shut your hole.
Sorry, I know you mean well, don't I?

She has poured herself another by now. She holds out her hand. He doesn't quite know what it's for. Then he realises that she wants him to hold it. He complies. They stay like this for a while; him standing there, and her drinking.
Eventually, TONI re-enters and breaks it up.
She is bright-eyed, almost perky. (She has taken cocaine).

TONI. That's better. I left my door open in case the phone, you know.

WENDY. That's right, Toni; I was going to say.

TONI. You never know; the Queen might have a rush of blood to the head.

WENDY. I think they've turned her down.

TONI. Fat lot of good's having a queen then, isn't it?

WENDY. Sorry, I've had a few.

TONI. That's what it's there for; I've got another bottle.

GEORGE. Yeah 'cos we couldn't find the duty-free at the . . .

TONI. No, I always pick up a couple of bottles when I'm on the move. I don't suppose you do cocaine, do you?

They look at her. They can't think of anything to say.

—No, I never used to—but since we went to live in Spain quite a lot of it seems to pass our way. I find it comes as quite a relief. Mother's little helper.

GEORGE. Tell you the truth, Toni, we don't really know what it is. I mean we don't sort of move in that realm, you know what I mean?

TONI. No, I just thought I'd offer. Just let me know if you want to do a line. (*Jauntily.*) As we say!

Pause.
They look at her, wondering about her.
She is detached, sniffing.

WENDY. All I can say is—I hope he had the guts to use that knife, take one of 'em with him. I do, honest.
Ah, what am I talking about? Don't pay no attention. What's the time?

GEORGE. Twenty-to.

They look at the TV.

WENDY. Television looks worse than ours, if that's possible. What I've seen of it. What's it like in Spain?

TONI. It's like having a hangover. We get *Dallas* and that sent out on video.

WENDY. Do you?

TONI. Yeah, daft isn't it?

GEORGE. No, not if you want to watch it.

TONI. I'm not bothered really. Not real, is it? No one lives like that.

GEORGE. No but I think a little bit of fantasy, it's all right. Harmless, isn't it?

Pause.
WENDY *has finished yet another drink. By this time* TONI *has noticed her drinking.*

TONI. I'd take it easy if I were you, love.

WENDY. You would, would you?

TONI. Yes I would.

GEORGE. Yeah, you know, Wend, because.

WENDY (*to* TONI). Well you're not, are you? You're not me. And you already said I was to help meself. This is *my* little helper.

TONI. I'm not being mean.

WENDY. That's all right then, isn't it?

WENDY has filled her glass again.

Cheers, eh? Here's to merry old Pe-nang. Arse-hole of the world where only turds can live.

She drinks.

—Wallop. Down the hatch. Eh George? Down the jolly old hatch.
Yes mate.

Pause.

—Anyway, better than killin' yourself on drugs, ennit?

TONI. I don't think there's a . . .

WENDY. No there *isn't* a lot of difference, is there? Is that what you were going to say?

TONI. Yeah.

WENDY. I thought so. Doctors give you pills, they ought to give you this. You've got to go with something, haven't you?

TONI. That's right.

WENDY. That's right. This is it. Know what I mean?

TONI. I thought you might want to keep a clear head because . . .

WENDY. What for? What for? What good's a clear head? Tell
    me—I'm really asking. Who wants to see things clearly?
    You'd fucking do yourself in, wouldn't you? No, mist it all
    up, mate. What are you doing?

    GEORGE *is looking through the mini-bar.*

GEORGE. We haven't touched nothing in here, Wendy. Here,
    d'you reckon they keep a check on how much of it you had?

TONI. Oh yes. They do that before you pay your bill.

GEORGE. Oh.

WENDY. I ain't paying my bleedin' bill.

GEORGE. They got lots of little miniatures and that . . . What's
    this? Vodka. Good for your nerves, that.

    He drinks it in one.

    —All on the *News of the World*, eh Wendy?
    What's this? Same again? Don't mind if I do.

    He drinks that too.

    —Funny drink, vodka. No wonder the Russkies are going to
    ban it, 'cos it drains the appetite to work. Cuts back the
    working-hours, sort of thing. Just the thing, really, ennit?
    Let's have a look . . .
    Dunno what that is but it's got to go the way of all the
    others.

    Drinks another.

    —Quite a bit in here, Wend, when you look.

TONI. You haven't got to drink all that; you've got the Scotch
    here.

GEORGE. No, I thought, a bit of variety, you know. Beer, that's
    boring, ennit?

    He continues knocking back the contents of the mini-bar.

WENDY (*meanwhile*). I know what I wanted to ask you, Toni. Lilly
    says you asked if she'd like to go out to Spain, is that right?

TONI. Well I said she could come and stay if she wanted.

WENDY. Stay?

TONI. Yes, once this is over and done with, if she felt like it.

WENDY. Yeah, but not anything longer, like?

TONI. Well, we didn't set a time, you know. Whatever holiday she gets.

WENDY. Well her whole life's a holiday—in time, anyway. Not so much otherwise.

TONI. Yes well, perhaps we ought to be thinking of the boys now, don't you think?

WENDY. Oh yeah.

There is an uneasy pause.

TONI. All right, come on; there's no point in dwelling on it.

WENDY. It's terrible—I know I should be thinking about him, but—my mind just sort of drifts, you know? It's terrible, isn't it?

TONI. It's because you're free, love.

WENDY. I don't feel it. No, it's just that she seems to be under the impression that you asked her for something more, you know. I don't know what she thinks, really, but she seemed to have the idea you was after a sort of live-in au pair or governess or something.

TONI. Oh.

WENDY. I thought it was a bit funny, but I never said nothing.

TONI. I don't think I would have said that, Wendy. Because I don't need anything like that.

WENDY. No, that's what I thought. She's probably made a mistake about how you live and that.

TONI. Yes.

WENDY. It's what I thought really, but I never said anything.

TONI. I've not got any children or anything.

WENDY. No.

TONI. Sorry if she's got the wrong idea.

WENDY. Well she . . . I don't know what she thinks, really.

TONI. I expect she's very upset.

WENDY. No, I haven't told her yet . . .

TONI. No I mean about her brother.

WENDY. Oh yes. Yes.

TONI. I'll straighten it out with her; don't worry.

WENDY. Mm. I ought to warn you—she's had quite a lot of
disappointments, one thing and another. You know, she
might *react*, sort of thing.

TONI. God it's so easy to raise people's expectations, isn't it?

WENDY. This is it.

TONI. I just don't need anything like that.

WENDY. No, that's what I thought.

TONI. I have a woman that comes in and does everything I need.
I just meant if she wants a break, you know. She could come
out and sit by the pool and all that.

WENDY. Yeah, well.

TONI. Same goes for you of course.

WENDY. Oh, right, yeah.

TONI. I thought it would take her mind off it all.

WENDY. Yeah, that's nice of you. Funny how we can sit here,
talking like this, isn't it? Nobody would believe it, would
they? Expect us to be—I dunno—wailing.

She drinks.

—It's all crap, isn't it? What they say in the papers.

TONI. I don't know about you but I'm glad of the company.

WENDY. Yeah. George is all right, but he's not really company,
you know.

TONI. That lawyer said she'd be with me but—it's not the same
with a foreigner, is it? They don't understand us, no matter
how educated they are.

WENDY. Well I'm sorry, I think if I saw that one again I'd
definitely kill her.

TONI. I think she was just a bit out of her depth really.

WENDY. Yeah well why did they give her a job like this? I mean it's too important to entrust to someone like that. They wanted to put a man on it. No one listens to a woman, and out here I expect it's even worse.

TONI. It's hard to take a woman doing that sort of job seriously. I mean they look daft in the clothes, for a start. I'm sorry but it's a fact of life. Women should stick to what they know best.

WENDY. That's right. God help us!

They both laugh—as best they can.
Silence as they look blankly at the TV.
GEORGE *is still at the mini-bar. He's had to accept the beer. He's pretty drunk by now.*

WENDY. You didn't bring that stuff in with you through the airport, did you Toni?

TONI. What stuff? Oh the coke. No love; I've never done that in my life. You can always score, no matter where you are.

WENDY. Good, 'cos I was going to say.

TONI. No, that would be the icing on the cake for this lot, wouldn't it? The mother an' all.

WENDY. Yeah they'd love that.

TONI. There's no shortage of offers on the street here.

WENDY. Doesn't it hurt your nose? I couldn't bear to put anything up my nose.

TONI. I've never thought about it really.

WENDY. I'd take heroin, you know.

TONI. You *would*, you say?

WENDY. Yes I've often thought about it. I never have taken drugs but I would take heroin. I wouldn't want to fart around with pot an' that—I'd go straight for the hard stuff.

WENDY *stops talking.*
TONI *watches her.*

GEORGE. Don't seem to be nothing else in here.

TONI. Oh yes, you can soon clear out a mini-bar.

GEORGE. Reduced to drinking beer, I am.

TONI. You can have a go at mine, if you like.

GEORGE. Can I?

TONI. If you want. I'm not touching mine.

GEORGE. Might take you up on that, Toni.

WENDY. If you can stand up.

GEORGE. 'Course I can stand up . . .

> *He staggers to his feet. But he looks lost and groggy. He stares at the TV. Then he picks up the bottle of Scotch. He looks at it for a second, as though it's an opponent; then he pours it down his throat. It is a joyless, desperate act.*
> *The women say nothing about it.*
> *He puts the bottle down.*

—Long time since I done that.

> *He slumps on to the bed.*

> *All of a sudden* LILLY *barges in from the next room. She is still not fully dressed and her mascara has run. But she doesn't care. She runs straight to* WENDY *and throws herself into her arms. It is a shock because she is too big for this sort of thing and also because there is clearly no common warmth of this kind amongst the family as a rule.*

WENDY. Oh, you *are* in there . . . Oi, mind me cigarette!

> LILLY *doesn't care about what an intrusion she's being. She sits or kneels still for some time, heaving a succession of sighs.* WENDY *comforts her.*
> TONI *watches.*

WENDY. It's all right, Lil, it's all right . . .

TONI. It's all right, pet.

WENDY. We're just amongst barbarians, that's all. We have to accept it. There's nothing we can do.

> LILLY *rises to her feet.*

LILLY (*finally*). All right Toni?

TONI. As well as can be expected, love.

LILLY. What's the matter with him?

WENDY. We're all having a drink.

> LILLY *looks around for a moment. Then she turns and goes quickly*
> *back to her room.*

TONI. She's an emotional lass, that one.

WENDY. She can be when she wants to be.

TONI. She's a real Cancer.

GEORGE (*wailing*). I worship the ground she walks on!

> *The two women look at one another.*
> *There is the suggestion of a smile.*

—I'd do anything for that girl. Swing for her, I would.

WENDY. Yeah well one's enough, ennit?
God, the things you find yourself saying.
You know what I said yesterday? I said we'll have a proper
holiday afterwards, with the money. I was meaning the
money we'll get from the papers, you know. It must have
sounded awful to her, 'cos she was around, you know—Miss
Snooty. But I didn't mean it like that; you just find yourself
saying things, don't you?

TONI. I know.

GEORGE. It's all right; it's only family talk.

WENDY. Oh you've revived, have you?
Anyway, who cares what she thinks. I doubt whether she's
even a proper lawyer. They probably just gave her the case
'cos she's no good. It was all cut and dried, wasn't it? Let's
face it—they never had a chance, did they?

TONI. I did think I could do something. But we're only human,
aren't we?

WENDY. Got your return ticket, have you?

TONI. Yes.

WENDY. That's good 'cos you don't want to hang around here,
do you?

TONI. I bought one outward and two home. (*She eats a nut.*)

WENDY. Oh.

TONI. So—if you know anyone that wants a one-way to Madrid.

GEORGE. You can get a refund on it, Toni.

WENDY. Tsk George!

GEORGE. She can. The hotel'll do it for her.

TONI. I'm happy to pay it. Pay it. It'll be the last expense I'll incur in that direction. I'll go home with an empty seat next to me. Can have a good old stretch out.

WENDY. It's a fucking farce, ennit?

She drinks.

TONI. She's got a nice side to her, your daughter.

WENDY. Lilly? Oh yeah. She keeps it hidden, but.

TONI. I should have liked a daughter, I think.

WENDY. Still not too late, is it?

TONI. No, I wouldn't want to go through all that. I mean someone I could talk to *now*. But then—I don't lead that kind of life really, I suppose.

WENDY. Why, what sort of a life you got to lead?

TONI. I've not even kept up with Ralph all these years. Because I don't want him to see what I'm doing. Not that I'm doing anything *terrible*, you know—but there's nothing like your own family to make you feel bad about things. No, I don't know how I'd go on with a teenage daughter; I'm probably all right as I am.

WENDY. Well you'll have to settle down, won't you Toni?

TONI. I expect I will love.

WENDY. It comes to us all, you know.

TONI. I know, but—I feel all my life as though nothing is real— and I'm sleepwalking through it.

WENDY. Yeah well it's all those drugs, isn't it?
You've got to be more like the rest of us, haven't you? Bored housewives an' that.

TONI. I don't like stepfathers for girls. I'm not settled with anyone, really, to tell you the truth. Not in my mind, like.

WENDY. You can't have everything, can you? I mean—I wouldn't mind living out in Spain and having a woman to come in and do for me, would I? But there you are: you can't have everything.

TONI. I'm not complaining.

WENDY. And daughters—I mean they talk to anyone but their mothers. I'm the last to hear of anything, I am. She defies her parents something awful, that girl.

TONI. She thinks the world of you.

WENDY. Oh yeah? She tell you that?

TONI *says nothing.*

—Got a funny way of showing it.

GEORGE. I think the world of that girl.

WENDY. Yeah we know, you'd do anything for her.

GEORGE. I would.

WENDY. Yeah.

GEORGE. I would.

WENDY. All right; we're impressed.

GEORGE. I know she ain't got nowhere to go 'cos I asked her and I know she'd be telling us left right and centre now if she had. Rubbing it in, she'd be.

He swings his legs off the bed.

—I think I feel a bit better now.

WENDY. Why, what have you done?

GEORGE. What time is it? Oh. (*Lights a cigarette.*) I worked in a pub once. I wasn't very old, was I Wend? 'Cos it was before we was married. Really rough part of King's Cross, it was. Bloke come in one night with a couple of mates. Really big bastard, he was, looked like a boxer or something. He had a wild look in his eye, looking for trouble, sort of thing. I served him. I could hear him saying to his mates: 'I feel like I'm gonna kill somebody tonight'. And it was like he really meant it, you know? You know when someone really means it. 'I'm gonna kill somebody tonight.' Anyway, I gave him his change and it was the one and only time in my life I done it, but I short-changed him, didn't I? It was a genuine mistake, like—but I went and short-changed him. God you should've seen the look on his face when he realised. Like I was a sort of sausage he wanted to chop up. I shall never forget that look. That's how I feel now, ennit? Like some big mean bastard's gonna come and chop me up.

TONI. They live very close to the edge, Scorpios. I always count my change. You have to in Spain; they'll try anything. They despise you if you don't.

GEORGE (*more to himself*). But I had to pick him see? Of all the people I might have made a mistake with—it had to be that big mean bastard.

TONI. Don't worry about it George. You can even get to enjoy being a Scorpio.

GEORGE. Eh, how d'you know I'm a Scorpio!

TONI. It's written all over your face.

GEORGE. Is it? What's she, then?

TONI (*frowning*). I don't know about Wendy. I don't like to make guesses.

WENDY. I don't know what I am, so you needn't worry.

GEORGE. November the 15th—that's when I was born. Is that Scorpio, is it? What, we like to sort of live dangerously, do we?

WENDY. He'll probably go off and get a job window-cleaning now.

GEORGE (*laughs to himself*). How about that? That's incredible, that is. I'm gonna go and get your mini-bar, if that's all right.

TONI. Help yourself, love. Drink the buggers dry, that's what I say.

GEORGE *staggers out.*

WENDY. You'd think they'd have something on the telly about it, though, wouldn't you? If only out of respect. I can't hardly believe it's happening.

TONI. I'd be very worried about you, Wendy.

WENDY. What? What d'you say?

TONI. I said I'd be very worried about you.

WENDY. You *would* be? How's that, then? Sorry, I'm not with you.

TONI. Perhaps it would be better if I said I *am* worried about you.

WENDY. What, just 'cos I said that about heroin? It was nothing—I think it's normal to want to try everything. See what all the fuss is about. Or you think I'm an alcoholic—is that it? Well it's not a big deal, is it? I mean how many alcos are there? Bet you're a bit of one. You can shift it; I seen you. Can you guess that sort of thing, or did I tell you? 'Cos I'm not a *bad* one; just an everyday one, you know what I mean? I just like a tipple every day; who doesn't if they're honest with theirselves? I did try to give it up once, mind, but I couldn't. Couldn't give it up. It hurt, trying. So I stopped trying and now I don't mind it. You live with it, don't you? You feel something coming on—you fight it or you—step inside of it. I sort of stepped inside of it and started living with it. It's not a big deal, is it?
You can see that in my face, can you?
I thought you was trying to sort of sus me out; I caught you looking at me a couple of times. It's all right; I don't mind. I'll tell you something, though, seriously. It isn't such a bad thing to be. It's the one thing in life you can sort of rely on. What I think is—so long as you're honest with yourself you're all right. Long as you don't tell yourself lies. I mean what's wrong with getting pissed? I'm not rolling around on the floor, you know. You'd hardly notice it. What I say is—all these things, they been put on earth for us to enjoy, so why not enjoy 'em? It's just killjoys with problems of their own want to stop you. That's what I think it is. We'd be all right if it weren't for people like that telling us how to behave. They wanna look after theirselves, instead of.
Fucking television, look at it. It's 24 hours now, isn't it? Must think we can't do without it. Must think we're all . . . They say it insults the intelligence—you heard 'em saying that? Makes me laugh, that does, 'cos if they asked me I'd tell 'em I *like* having my intelligence insulted. Why shouldn't it be? *I'm* insulted, aren't I? Every day. Do you know what I do for a living, Toni? Did I tell you? Bet you can't read this in my face or whatever it is. I go to a canteen in Malet Street; I

stand there in this stupid turban-thing and I say 'Custard or cream? Custard or cream . . .?' (*She repeats it a number of times.*) You've no idea what a twat I feel. I mean I'm only waiting for the day I'm replaced by a fucking parrot. But there you are. The question has to be asked, doesn't it? Otherwise how's anyone gonna know whether they can have it, custard or cream? They can have a choice, you see? That's very important for people, that is. If some twat don't ask the question—well, I mean, it's complete and utter chaos, ennit? The whole system breaks down. You can say something now.

TONI. They should have self-service.

WENDY. Ah but I wouldn't have the job then, would I? Then we'd both be out of work, me *and* him. See, that remark it's typical of someone that don't know. 'They should have self-service.' Maybe they ought *but what about me?* I mean up the workers and all that. That's typical, that is. I mean why not everything machines? Do without us altogether. Why not? I don't need to stand there like a twat, do I? They ought to pay me for stopping indoors, didn't they?

TONI. People have to work somewhere.

WENDY. Exactly, they do, don't they? Bastards have to if they want their little luxuries. Soft toilet paper, a little day out. A tree at Christmas, a bit of 'olly on it. This is the first holiday I've had in ten years—do you believe that?

TONI. I think people complain too much in England.

WENDY. Cor, you're probably gonna say Mrs Thatcher's doing a good job in a minute.

TONI. I don't like her as a person but I do admire her.

WENDY. Yeah, me an' all. She sorts 'em out, don't she? I voted for her, didn't I? George never, but I did. Fuck all she's done for us, though.

TONI. I think she's probably tried her best.

WENDY. Anyway, you're quite right—I *do* complain. What's more, I ain't gonna stop. Anyway, what do you do that's so clever, you haven't got to slave away like the rest of us?

TONI. Don't worry, love, I work.

WENDY. What at then?

TONI. I married a crook, love.

WENDY. Well that ain't work, marrying somebody.

TONI. All right.

WENDY. I mean, is it? Any pratt could do that. I think I did actually but look where it's got me.

TONI. I don't work in a canteen, I grant you that.

WENDY. No, I was just saying.

TONI. It's the only way you can get anything these days, and hold on to it. There's no money in being honest.

WENDY. Sorry, but I find that attitude's exactly what's wrong with England today.

TONI. Do you?

WENDY. No.

They both laugh.

TONI. Everyone says they miss it, England. The green fields and the brown cows and the sausages and the football and the autumn. Not me, I don't miss a damn thing. Never look back, me.

WENDY. I never look forward. What's there to look forward to?

TONI. Don't ask me.

WENDY. Oh I thought you was a sort of an agony aunt, like they have in the *TV Times*.

TONI. No.

WENDY. Oh, I must have been misinformed.

TONI. The only thing I do know is—you've got to take risks. Calculated risks.

WENDY. God that's all I need, ennit?

TONI. Anyway, Wendy, this is hardly the day to go into our . . .

WENDY. IT NEVER IS THE DAY!
Sorry, it's 'cos I've had a few. Usually I can hold it. Straight, I can drink a bottle of that stuff and you wouldn't know it. That boy of yours killed my Bryan. Bryan took a risk, didn't he? He could easily have given that ticket to someone else,

said it was too much for him, but he didn't—he took a risk
and it killed him. I could kill you. I might yet. 'Cos you're a
pusher, just like him. That girl's not going within an inch of
your place. Cocaine and your boy's about to be hanged for
drugs! Excuse me, but I think that's very sick.
Fuck this big mouth of mine. But I mean it. Well—no I don't
mean it. I'm sorry, I don't know what I do mean. I don't
know.

TONI *puts her arms round her.*
Silence.
The lights go down on the hotel room.
Another part of the stage:
The prison cell.
RALPH *and* BRYAN, *chained and dressed for execution. With
them, the* GAOLER *and (if possible) various other officials.*

GAOLER. All right, Bryan, is there anything I can do for you
before you go off?

BRYAN *shakes his head.*

—Ralph? Is there anything I . . .?

RALPH (*suddenly*). No! No, nothing. Yes! I'd like to see Paris
before I die. (*He laughs*). No one gets it! It's a *line*, man. It's a
line from a W.C. Fields movie. W.C. Fields—great movie star.
No one knows! I'm dying amongst fools.

GAOLER. Just wait a . . .

But RALPH *is starting to have a fit. He goes berserk. The* GAOLER
grabs the chain and dodges around with RALPH. RALPH *is not
trying to hit anyone; he is like a crazy man having a fit. He can't
control any of his movements, or his voice. He cries out No, no, no! etc.
All this time,* BRYAN *watches, completely still and silently aghast. He
smokes his cigarette. It goes on for some time.*
RALPH *is eventually restrained—or the fit burns itself out. He gets to
his feet. No one speaks for a while.* RALPH *continues to shake.*
The GAOLER *appears to be awaiting a signal from somewhere.*

RALPH (*inaudibly*). How's the cigarette?

BRYAN. What?

RALPH. How's the cigarette?

BRYAN. It's all right.

RALPH. Is it?

BRYAN. Yeah.

RALPH. Shouldn't smoke, get cancer. Call that gallows humour, you heard of that? You know what I'm talking about?

BRYAN says nothing.

I can't free my hands. I'm never gonna see my hands again. Jesus, I love my body. Love every inch of it. My lovely, precious body.

Pause.

BRYAN. Oi.
Here's another fine mess you've gotten me into.

They both laugh.

GAOLER. OK boys. Say goodbye please.

RALPH. Goodbye.

BRYAN. 'Bye.

They go to each other and embrace as best they can. BRYAN *is very still.*

The scene ends.

Lights up again on the hotel room.
TONI *still has her arms around* WENDY.
They separate. Then enter GEORGE. *He staggers in carrying* TONI's *mini-bar. He puts it on top of his own.*

WENDY. You didn't have to bring the whole thing in.

GEORGE. I want to see what's in it, don't I?

WENDY. Well you could've done that in there.

GEORGE. Yeah well, you know . . .

WENDY. Oh please yourself, you want to give yourself a hernia, that's your look-out.

GEORGE. Let's see . . . Eh, they've given her lots more than they give us.

TONI. They must have been anticipating my requirements.

WENDY. God I ought to be there! What am I doing? Don't you think? I mean, just because I didn't want to be photographed, that ain't a reason, is it?

TONI. You wouldn't do any good, love.

WENDY. No but at least I'd be there, wouldn't I? God, that's me, that is. Always in the wrong place.

TONI. That's why they hang men. Because it upsets the women. Don't give them the satisfaction.

GEORGE. You wouldn't want them all staring at you on the telly, would you?

WENDY. Yeah but it's my boy, ennit? Comes to something when you can't put yourself out a bit. I mean I ain't gonna do anything for him again, am I? Couldn't I get one of them rickshaw-things? They understand English, don't they?

She waits for them to answer, but they don't. Besides, she doesn't make any move and soon seems to forget her suggestion.

GEORGE. Gin that must be.

WENDY. What you drinking that stuff for?

GEORGE. It's the mini-bar, Wendy.

WENDY. I know what it is; I'm saying—it's *theirs*, ennit? What you drinking their liquor for when we got our own?
(*To* TONI). He can't hold his drink, see.

TONI. Let's kill the bottle, shall we?

WENDY. Thought I already had.

They drink.

TONI. Queen's messenger on his white horse is what we want now.

WENDY. Useless fucking Queen. Probably sitting under a pile of dogs, and them stupid sons of hers. God, don't you hate 'em all?

TONI (*unsure*). Well . . .

GEORGE. The Royal children, you know, they're brought up with special trousers—they got no pockets in 'em. It's so they can't put their hands in their pockets. Did you know that?

WENDY. What you drinking?

GEORGE. Dunno, haven't got me glasses!

They both laugh and cough.

WENDY. He always says that: what you drinking? Dunno, ain't got me glasses.

GEORGE. It's especially poignant in my case 'cos it's true.

WENDY. Get him—'poignant'. What's that mean?

GEORGE. Means poignant, dunnit?

WENDY. Yeah I know but what's it *mean?*

GEORGE. Means what it sounds like.

WENDY. Sounds like you're pissed, mate.

GEORGE. That's true.

WENDY. You're pissed, amigo. Isn't he Toni?
I suppose some people live like this all the time, don't they? I don't think you can make money if you're honest. That's what I think. What do you think?

TONI. Mm.

WENDY. I don't think you can. Government's got it all worked out, haven't they? You make a square bob and—wallop; they're on to you. What's your racket, darlin'?

TONI. Oh I don't know.

WENDY. Oh yeah, you married well, didn't you? That's it? See, you didn't ought to say things like that; you didn't ought to put yourself down.

TONI. I haven't got a racket of my own, love.

WENDY. Yeah but you're not short of a bob or two, are you?

TONI. I manage.

WENDY. Yeah you're a glamorous woman. Ain't she George?

GEORGE. What's that?

WENDY. I'm saying Toni here—she's a glamorous woman?

TONI. Shut up, love, for God's sake.

WENDY. Yeah, all right.

TONI. Don't take your frustrations out on me. You've got a lot of good qualities—use them and stop complaining. I've never heard anyone complain so much as the English.

WENDY. Maybe we got a lot to complain about.

TONI. But you've not been anywhere. Have you? You've not seen anywhere else, to compare yourself with.

WENDY. Bryan went somewhere, didn't he? Look what happened to him.
(*Suddenly to* GEORGE.) For God's sake, will you stop drinking them fucking things!

She snatches one of the bottles from him and hurls it across the room.

—I keep hearing this bloody unscrewing sound; it's driving me fucking mad. If you're gonna drink, drink like a man.

GEORGE. Right.

He stands up, but almost immediately sinks down again.

—Oh dear . . .

WENDY. Christ—it's not funny, is it? (*To* TONI.) Do you find this amusing at all?

TONI. No.

WENDY. Neither do I. How did we get started? I didn't even notice it starting. What time is it? What are we doing here?

TONI. We're taking our minds off it.

WENDY. Yeah. Some joke, ennit?

GEORGE. I'm gonna kill someone tonight.

LILLY *bursts in again. She still isn't fully-dressed. In her forearm, a needle is sticking out.*

LILLY (*to* GEORGE). Gonna kill someone are you? That's nice. How about me?

She moves downstage holding out her arm, for everyone to see.

—Here you are. This is my poison—what's yours?

She sniffs the glass.

—Hm, whisky.

Didn't know I was on this, did you? Been on it for a year now.

TONI (*quietly*). God, get that needle out of her arm.

WENDY. I ain't touching it. Oh Christ.

LILLY (*laughs*). !!

> TONI *goes to take out the needle.*

—It's all right; I can manage.

> *She withdraws the needle, rubs her arm then flings the needle across the room.*

—It's good stuff they got out here; I can recommend it.

> GEORGE *has staggered to his feet. He reaches her and raises a fist. She doesn't flinch. But the punch never comes. He falls first or else it's a completely innocuous punch.*
> *She laughs.*

WENDY. Actually I *did* know you were on it . . .

LILLY. Bollocks, you never . . .

WENDY. . . . But I didn't say anything.

LILLY. You always got to know everything, you have, haven't you?

WENDY. But I don't see why you've got to shock us with it.

GEORGE. I didn't know.

WENDY. I suppose you want to get us all in there with Bryan, do you? Eh? Trying to get us all busted?

LILLY. She knows all the phrases, don't she? 'Busted'.

> WENDY *slaps her round the face, hard.*

—That hurt.

WENDY. Where do you get this from?

LILLY. What difference does it make?

WENDY. Do you know?

TONI. I've got an idea. It wasn't from me, if that's what you're thinking.

WENDY. And you want a daughter? Christ, have this one—she's been nothing but heartache to me.

LILLY. Gary got me on it; he was a pusher, wasn't he?

WENDY. Charming boy. Puts her in the hospital and gets her on H. She'd be better off where you live, amongst the crooks.

LILLY. What difference does it make? (*She switches channels on the radio.*)—Any music on this?

GEORGE. I'm not in the mood for music, Lil.

She carries on. The music obscures some of TONI's *remarks on the phone.*

TONI (*on telephone*). Hello Room Service. Can you send up the barman please? . . . To Room 433. I want the barman from the International Bar . . . Yes, if that's his name. Straight away.

WENDY. You're not sharing them needles, I hope. You hear me?

LILLY. Yeah, I heard. I don't share nothing. It's the way I was brought up. Anyway, I got lots of needles.

GEORGE. I'm gonna fucking kill this—bottle.

He drinks lustily. Afterwards he is almost paralytic.

WENDY. I suppose you think you're clever?

LILLY. You didn't half hurt me then.

WENDY. You think it's shocking or something.

LILLY. Well, I'll tell you—you should of seen the look on your face.

WENDY. You slut.

LILLY. Takes one to know one, dunnit? All right, Toni? All set to go, I am! Viva Espana, eh? It's all right, I'm not usually like this. I can behave myself usually, can't I Mummy dear?

WENDY. Where is it?

LILLY. Where's what?

WENDY. This stuff—where is it?

LILLY. Why—who's coming?

WENDY. I want to try it.

LILLY. You? (*Laughs*.)

WENDY. What's so funny?

LILLY. You wanna try it?

WENDY. Yeah, me.

LILLY (*to* TONI). What's she on about?

TONI. It's nothing to do with me, love.

WENDY (*moving to* LILLY's *room*). Where is it . . .?

LILLY. Eh, hang on . . . You haven't got no idea!

> WENDY *goes into the next room, followed by* LILLY. LILLY *has found music on the TV. It remains on—not loud as yet. It is crude Malaysian rock.*
> TONI *sits still with her drink.* GEORGE *is lying on the floor (or the bed).*
> *After a while, a knock on the door and the* BARMAN *comes in. He is in his off-duty clothes, dressed like a young stud.*

TONI. Yes, come in please. Well you've been putting yourself about, haven't you?

BARMAN. Huh?

TONI. Did you sell that young lady some smack?

BARMAN. I don't know what you're talking about.

> *Pause.*
> *They look at each other.*
> *He turns to go; she stops him.*
> *He reacts—he doesn't like being touched.*

BARMAN. OK, what d'you want—go to your room?

TONI. No thank you. It's a charming offer, mind.

BARMAN. Room Service said you wanted me, so I don't know. I don't sell no smack. We can talk it over in your room—OK.

TONI. Real little animal, aren't you? I think my husband could use a man like you.

> LILLY *comes in again.*

LILLY. Here he is—Fu Man Chu. Hi man! (*She smiles and mimes injecting needle into arm.*)

BARMAN. I don't know what she's talking about.

TONI. It's all right; we're not going to report you. Did you think we were going to report you?
No, we've asked you to come and dance for us. Haven't we Lilly?

LILLY. Have we? Yeah.

TONI. He's going to give us a dance, 'cos we're on holiday.

LILLY. He's got a lot of different talents hasn't he?

TONI. Yes, I bet he's a lovely mover. I bet he's got pictures of John Travolta on his wall.

LILLY. Yeah look at all his gold—you could melt him down and make a bob or two, couldn't you?

TONI. Yeah.

> The BARMAN *makes an ambiguous gesture to* TONI—*it could be a pass.*

> TONI *suddenly slaps him fiercely. He reacts, but checks himself.* TONI *laughs at him. Even* LILLY *is surprised.*

—Fancy yourself, don't you?

BARMAN. I gotta go.

TONI. No, you haven't. You stop here, love. You're in demand. You go back and you won't have a job to go to. Straight into prison, savvy? No, you're going to give Lilly and me a little dance.

BARMAN. I go to gaol, you go to gaol too.

TONI. It's all right by me. (*She smiles sweetly at him*).

BARMAN. You're crazy, you know that?

TONI. That's me, love, crazy lady. Turn the music up Lilly.

BARMAN. OK, who gives a fuck?

LILLY. Oh that's something else he promised to do for me an' all.

TONI. Yes I thought so.

LILLY. Fair dos he's not bad, is he?

TONI. Come on—let's see you move it.

The BARMAN *starts to dance, watched by* TONI *and* LILLY. *He gets into it. He's good and he knows it.*

WENDY *comes in again. She is grasping her arm. Blood is running down it, from the vein. She stands there, rocking on her feet.*

At one point, LILLY *springs up and plants a huge kiss on the* BARMAN's *lips. Then she goes and sits and watches him again. The music continues; the* BARMAN *dances.*

At the end, they are in the following positions, perhaps frozen:

TONI *is sitting on the bed, looking right through the* BARMAN, *and beyond.*

GEORGE *is grappling like a drowning man at* WENDY. *He succeeds in pulling her down. They collapse together.*

LILLY, *unable to control herself any more, makes a rush at the* BARMAN *and plunges her hand inside his trousers. She throws her head back in silent laughter. The* BARMAN *raises her arms.*

The LAWYER *enters. She appears to have something to say, but she is stopped in her tracks by the scene in front of her.*

A split-second after the LAWYER's *entrance, two hoodied bodies are hanged. The sound of their fall echoes.*

Lights out quickly.

End

MICHAEL WALL

Michael Wall was born in Herefordshire, and attended the University of York, 1973–6. He now lives and works in London. He has spent a lot of time travelling and much of the material for his plays is taken from his experiences abroad. He has written a number of radio plays, including *The Wide-Brimmed Hat, Headcrash* (banned by Radio 4) and *Hiroshima: The Movie* (winner of a Sony Award and a Giles Cooper Award). For the stage he has written *Japanese Style*, based on his experiences as an English teacher in Japan, *Imaginary Wars in England*, about a right-wing coup in England, and *Blue Days*, a comedy about the 'nouveaux-riches' in Spain. *Amongst Barbarians* won him the Mobil Prize in 1988.